Profitable Crafts Marketing

PROFITABLE CRAFTS MARKETING

*A Complete Guide
to
Successful Selling*

Brian T. Jefferson

TIMBER PRESS
Portland, Oregon
1985

DEDICATION

I firmly believe that every creative person benefits by having a mentor, a person who supports, encourages, questions and listens. A person who says "Go ahead and try it. So what if it doesn't work. You can always try something else."

This book is dedicated to my mentor, friend and wife, Judy. Her unquestioning support has allowed me to dream dreams and achieve them. I hope that I have done the same for her.

© Timber Press 1985

Printed in the United States of America.
ISBN 0-88192-013-4

TIMBER PRESS
P.O. Box 1631
Beaverton, Oregon 97075

Contents

PART FOUR: OTHER PROFITABLE MARKETING CHANNELS

Acknowledgements

I would like to thank all the craftspeople that I have known and worked with. Without their dedication and love for their chosen work, this book would not have been possible.

My daughters, Kristin and Rachel deserve thanks for putting up with my hours at the typewriter, while their friends' dads were out doing "real work."

A salute to Joe Gilman who has helped many with the craftsmanship of living.

Finally, thanks to Richard Abel, my editor, for helping transform the original manuscript into its current state. In my work as a professor I do a goodly amount of editing of papers, manuscripts and theses, and quite frankly it was a little difficult to reverse roles and get edited, but Richard did it with sympathy and understanding and patience, and for that I am grateful.

This book was made possible in part by a grant from the Georgia Council for the Arts through the appropriations from the Georgia General Assembly and the National Endowment for the Arts.

PART ONE

Marketing Theories
and Strategies

Chapter 1

Introduction to Crafts Marketing

This book is about crafts marketing and is designed for serious craftsmen who want to learn more about effective ways to sell their product.

Making a living as a craftsman is not an easy endeavor, but it is possible and can be extremely rewarding if you have an effective marketing program. It may require a change of attitude towards crafts and the business of selling them. The great majority of craftsmen make crafts because it gives them pleasure, a sense of accomplishment, a feeling of worth. Only secondarily do they think of marketability. In the business community the exact opposite is true. Marketability is the first consideration and in some cases the only consideration. In the traditional business community the motto is "Find a need and fill it." In the world of the craftsman it, too often, is "I'll make what I want and then see if anyone wants to buy it."

I.B.M. is one of the largest corporations in the world. It got to that position because of its marketing plan. I know that you don't want to be another I.B.M., but you do want to grow and prosper in your business. Listen to what the experts say about I.B.M. I.B.M. does not have the best equipment, is not the most innovative, and does not develop new products as frequently as other companies. In fact they often wait until a product is developed and tested in the market before they come out with a similar product. The secret to I.B.M.'s success is a marketing team that sincerely believes in their products and goes out and sells the hell out of them.

The secret to your success? Believe in your product and sell the hell out of it! Many craftsmen have failed in the craft business because they have been unable, or unwilling, to deal with the realities of the business world. Others have failed or have barely survived because they didn't want to sacrifice the integrity of their craft. If you have those same feelings, you'll need to change your attitude.

Please note that I didn't say anything about changing your craft! In fact, in most instances you can continue making the crafts you currently make and significantly increase your sales simply by using effective marketing techniques.

So, a marketing plan doesn't force you to do anything radical at all. It simply asks you to view your craft the way the consumer views it and to provide a means to trade your product for the consumer's money. Instead of doing what you want, you are meeting the needs and wants of the customer. But you'll still be doing what you want because you'll still be making crafts, although you'll probably be making a lot more money at it.

I advocate a targeted marketing approach, believing that nobody can succeed, particularly in the craft business, trying to be everything to everybody. The book uses a targeted approach in helping you do one thing: market your craft more effectively and more profitably.

Here are some of the topics that will be covered:

1. How to evaluate the effectiveness of various marketing channels.
2. How to test market your craft.
3. How to determine which products sell best in which markets.
4. How to determine your profit on each item sold.
5. What to do if a craft item is not selling.
6. How to predict market trends.
7. How to develop new products to meet consumer demand.
8. How to appeal to consumer wants.
9. How a targeted marketing plan can assure business growth.

A targeted marketing system approach to marketing is an aggressive, well planned and well tested strategy for presenting your product in the marketplace. It means that you don't take January, February and March off waiting for the fairs to start again. It means that you will use these months to exhibit at wholesale shows or to concentrate on mail order (January, February and March are the highest sales volume months). It means that you will have a marketing strategy that will take advantage of the most profitable marketing channels at the most profitable times.

Nobody can tell you exactly what your marketing system will look like when it is developed, but you can be sure that it will fit your particular needs and that it will keep your business growing as long as you keep your system up to date. It will be hard work, but if you are serious about being in the crafts business you must realize from the start that no item that you make will sell well indefinitely and no item will sell well in every market channel. An effective marketing system will constantly keep you informed about how each item is selling in each marketing area, which items have increased in sales, which have decreased, and what the demand will be for your products in the future.

The book is divided into five parts:

1. Marketing Theories and Strategies
2. Retail Marketing Methods
3. Wholesale Marketing Methods
4. Other Profitable Marketing Channels
5. Professional Concerns

In Part One you'll learn about basic marketing terms and how they apply to you. You'll learn how to determine from the beginning whether a craft item will be profitable and in which market channel it will be most profitable. You'll be shown how to position your product so that you can find the right hole in the marketplace and how to develop new accounts and maintain old ones.

Part Two concentrates on analyzing the advantages and disadvantages of selling in retail market channels. In each market outlet you'll be shown how to: enter the market, deal with your competition, develop effective marketing strategies, price for the market, determine legal obligations and analyze the potential profitability.

Part Three focuses on wholesale marketing and volume selling techniques. You'll get an overview of successful wholesale selling strategies and then will learn how to use them whether you are selling to a shop, gallery, at a wholesale craft show or to a department store.

Part Four deals with other profitable marketing outlets such as commissions, mail order and unusual market channels. You'll learn how important it is to design your marketing effort for a specific marketing channel.

Part Five discusses professional concerns such as having a sound business plan, working with an agent, what to do if your work isn't selling and protecting yourself through copyright.

The Appendix lists helpful people and organizations that can assist you in developing your business and includes the three most important legal contracts you need as a craftsman.

Like any good marketing plan, you need to know where you are going and how you are going to get there. Hopefully this introduction has served to give you an overview of what this book is all about, but no plan works until you put it in action. Let's get started!

Chapter 2

Marketing Principles for the Craftsman

Marketing is not a mysterious process engaged in by a select few corporate types called marketing managers. In fact, everyone engages in marketing activities on a daily basis, almost as soon as they are born. Babies crying because they are hungry are demonstrating that they have a need that they want filled. They reward the person filling that need by stopping their crying. Thus, marketing is an exchange process, in which the person with the greatest need usually initiates the process. In our example, the baby is the initiator because he has the greatest need. In crafts marketing the crafts producer (you) is almost always the initiator because he needs to sell his products to recover his invested capital to make more and pay his bills.

If you need to sell 1,000 widgets a month in order to make your crafts business a success, then it is up to you to undertake the marketing effort required to achieve your goal. The various kinds of sales efforts you make constitute your marketing plan. A marketing plan can be organized and efficient, or haphazard and wasteful.

To begin, let's review some of the common marketing concepts so that you will be able to apply them to the specific marketing channels you choose to develop in your marketing plan.

☐ MARKETING CONCEPTS

There are universal marketing concepts that apply whether you are selling crafts, gourmet jelly beans or real estate. Understanding the principles will assist you in selecting the right marketing approach for your unique craft products.

Exchange Potential

If you have a product and someone wants or needs that product, you have all the ingredients for exchanging your product for suitable consideration (money). Some products, like food and shelter, have high exchange potential because these are things that people have to have. Crafts have a lower exchange potential, but that can be overcome.

Marketing Strategies

Anything you do to get the buyer and the seller (you) together for the purpose of exchanging valuables (your crafts for his money) is defined as a marketing strategy. There are many strategies available to you as a craftsperson, some more effective than others.

Obstacles to Selling

If you have a product and somebody wants it, you expect an easy sale, but that isn't necessarily the case! Marketing specialists agree that roadblocks to completing even the easiest sale exist. They place these roadblocks in five different categories: space, time, knowledge, value and ownership. Here's how they affect you:

Space. A craftsman carving Eskimo sculptures out of whale bone in the frozen wastes of Alaska has a space problem if he cannot find a way to get his product to buyers in New York, Chicago and San Diego. One solution would be to wholesale the work to galleries so that people interested in buying his work have readier access to it.

Time. Buyers want something when they want it. If it is not available, they will buy something else or simply not spend any money. A simple solution is to maintain a full inventory of all objects you make at all times. Demand is also seasonal, so you should build larger inventories for high demand times such as Christmas.

Knowledge. If people don't know you exist or what product you make, you cannot expect them to beat down the door to buy. Billions of dollars are spent each year on advertising to acquaint people with products and services. Obviously, you will not spend as much as General Mills, but advertising should be part of your marketing strategy.

Value. The value you place on your craft item (the price) may not be what the buyer or potential buyer places on it. If that is the case, you have two choices:

1. Lower your price to what the buyer thinks it should be.
2. Educate the buyer as to why the product is really worth the price you are asking for it.

Ownership. Unless the buyer can be persuaded to give you something of value for your product, no exchange of ownership takes place. Offering credit card service, accepting checks or providing installment payment plans all help to facilitate ownership.

□ MARKETING FUNCTIONS

Any marketing strategy serves only one purpose: to overcome obstacles to selling. Think about that for a moment. Any marketing plan you develop must be organized upon and around marketing functions that are the most successful in facilitating the sale of your crafts. The marketing functions you need to consider are:

Market Analysis

This is where the "Find a need and fill it" axiom comes in.

Anything you do to determine whether anyone is interested in your product, where they live, what their income is etc., etc., comes under the heading of market analysis. Unfortunately, not many craftspeople use market analysis techniques as effectively as they might and some don't use them at all.

Market Communications

Anything you do to make people more aware of you and your product is market communication. Advertising in newspapers, magazines, radio, TV, direct mail campaigns and sponsoring hot air balloon races are all examples of market communications.

Remember that communication is a two-way process. In addition to telling people about your product, *listen* to what they are saying about your product. It could very well mean the difference between your success or failure.

Product Differentiation

What can you do to make your product more appealing and distinguish it from similar products? Can you change the color or offer a choice of colors, change the package or the message, raise or lower the price? The purpose of differentiation is to have your product stand out. Calvin Klein used this principle in marketing his jeans, as did Chiquita with bananas and Atari with computer games.

Market Selection

Nobody has ever produced a product that appealed to everyone, *ever!* Therefore, you need to find that group of people most likely to buy your product. Your research may reveal that 78% of the people who buy your product are female and under 30 years old. You obviously have a target group that you can concentrate your efforts on. It normally doesn't come that easily, but you can identify your buying public to some extent and thus make more effective use of your advertising dollars.

I worked with one craftsman who was making a line of hardwood kitchen items — rolling pins, cutting boards, recipe boxes, bowls, etc., etc. Kitchen items are of interest to a wide segment of the population, but we worked out a marketing plan that would attract gourmet cooks because they had the interest and financial resources necessary to buy his beautifully made, but rather expensive, one-of-a-kind items.

Valuation Function

This category deals with cost and perceived value. Any time a buyer purchases a product, whether a hand-thrown stoneware mug or a $200,000 house, he does so because the value to him meets or exceeds the price he has to pay. If the value of an item is not perceived as equal to or greater than the price, he will not buy it.

A classic example of the valuation function in reverse is found in the automobile industry. The high price of cars combined with high interest rates caused a dramatic decline in sales. Why? Because people are saying, "Sure, I'd like a new car, but I'm not going to pay $250 a month for it." They are not willing to sacrifice that much for a new car so the value to them is less than the cost. Result? They don't buy. Automobile manufacturers offered interest rates below the prime for new car buyers. The result? Greatly increased sales.

Exchange Function
This function deals with any action designed to facilitate the sale. If you offer galleries a discount for prompt payment, you are providing an exchange function. If you accept credit cards or personal checks you are again providing an exchange function. Churches pass collection plates at services and charities solicit for funds, both exchange function. The bottom line is that you must provide services that make it easy for the buyer to pay for your product.

☐ MARKETING GUIDELINES

Marketing has been around for thousands of years and will play a major function in our society as long as there are people with wants and people to fill those wants. Buyers and sellers adhere to established marketing laws that are as useful today as they were in Caesar's day. Here they are:
1. As a producer, you find a need or want and fill it.
2. As a consumer, you define your needs and wants and then find others to fill them.
3. Marketing describes the effort needed to satisfy both wants and needs. People need only the bare essentials of food, water, and shelter. People want much, much more, so marketing is concerned with filling people's wants.
4. Your business will grow as the want or need for your product increases and will decline as the want or need declines.
5. Businesses succeed in spite of falling demand by adapting to satisfy new or different wants.
6. A product is what a customer perceives it to be, not what it actually is.
7. People's wants are endless; you are competing against all the other uses for people's money, so you must market constantly.
8. Give consumers what they want. Find out what they *will* buy, not what they *say* they will buy.

☐ THE LAW OF SUPPLY AND DEMAND

One of the principle rules of economics is: the higher the price, the lower the demand and the lower the price the higher the demand. You and I know, however, that in the crafts business the principle does not always apply — it all has to do with perceived value.
As a craftsman you need to keep in mind that the consumer has the final say as to what price is acceptable, sometimes forcing you to find production methods that will be more cost effective. In other

words, you will need to do some testing to see what customers will pay and what you need to charge to obtain a reasonable profit.

Naturally, as a businessman, you will want to make a fair profit. If you can sell a wooden toy for $20 and make a good profit, you will plan to make a lot of them. If, on the other hand, you can get only $5 for the same toy, receiving little or not profit, you won't be eager to produce too many. Here's what it looks like in graph form:

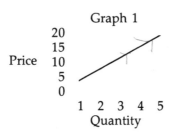

Graph 1

We see that at a price of $5 you produce very few, but at $20 you produce many more.

However, the higher the price of your product, the lower the demand, as illustrated in the next graph (Graph 2).

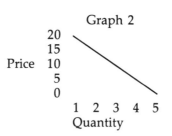

Graph 2

Here we see that theoretically you can sell 5 items at $5 for every one you can sell at $20.

Remember that the desired goal is to produce enough products to meet the demand. If we combine the two as in Graph 3, we arrive at a price that will allow supply and demand to equalize.

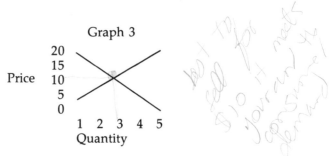

Graph 3

In this illustration we see that at a selling price of $12.50, you can sell everything you make and still show a profit; in other words, supply has matched demand. This is the goal you should always strive for.

Remember, though, it is the consumer who ultimately determines the value of a product. As long as demand remains high you can charge high prices for your work. But at some point (if you continue to raise your prices to meet demand) the cost of your product will exceed its value to some fraction of your customers and demand will drop, often suddenly.

We are all familiar with the rapid rise in the cost of imported fuel oil. Recently, prices began to drop. Why? Because the price had risen so high that people finally began to conserve through car pools, public transportation and buying more fuel efficient cars. The result? An oil surplus created by reduced demand resulting in lower prices.

Another excellent example is the computer industry. Personal computers have become extremely popular because the price has continued to drop putting them within the means of the average American family.

☐ A MARKETING MODEL FOR THE CRAFTSMAN

Any marketing plan must be organized and must be tailored to fit the individual craftsman. Let's say, for example, that a craftsman makes wooden toys in his house. He knows that in addition to selling directly from his studio he needs additional craft outlets in order to make the amount of money he requires. He knows the six marketing functions: market analysis, market communication, product differentiation, market selection, valuation function and exchange function and he has plans to use all of them in his marketing strategy. He also knows that he will have some obstacles to overcome and he lists these as space, time, knowledge, value and ownership. In order to get an idea of what he's up against, he draws a chart that looks like this:

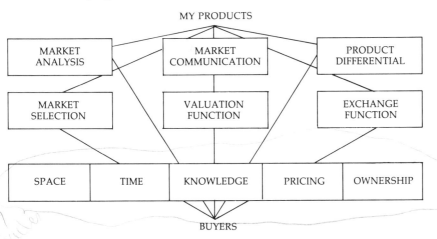

After completing the chart he summarizes his task and realizes that in order to get his product to his customers he will need to find ways to:

1. Get his products from the studio to the buyer.
2. Find a way to have his product available when the buyer wants it.
3. Keep buyers informed about his products.
4. Price his products fairly so that the buyer receives perceived value for his money.
5. Promote the uniqueness of his product.
6. Provide ways to make it easy for the customer to buy his product.

These six marketing concerns hold true regardless of which marketing channel you choose. However, different emphasis will be assigned to each marketing function depending on the market channel you select. For example, mail order marketing depends heavily on advertising (market communication) while wholesale selling requires attention to terms (exchange function).

□ SELECTING YOUR MARKET(S)

An essential part of any marketing strategy is selecting your market. A market, for our purposes, is a particular group of people who would benefit from your product. People who attend craft fairs, shop at galleries, wear designer clothes, invest in art or buy through mail order are all potential markets as are many, many others.

Some products have such universal appeal or demand that a broad-based approach to marketing can be adopted. Manufacturers of aspirin, deodorant, soft drinks and other such products don't bother to identify such specialized markets.

Most businesses (including yours) must use a targeted market approach. This means that you first identify all your potential buyers and then divide them into subgroups or market segments. The idea is to identify the subgroups to which you will market your products, using a different marketing technique to reach each unique group. I recommend that you use a three-step approach to identifying your market group.

1. Describe the total market for your product. At this stage it includes all the market channels that are traditionally used by craftsmen plus any others that you can think of.
2. Divide the market up into logical segments. You may decide at this stage that the markets that have the most potential for you are: the fair, the mall show, direct sales from the studio and mail order.
3. Arrange the segments into market potential priorities. You may decide that you need to get maximum exposure of your craft so you assign number one priority to the fair, second to the mall show, third to mail order and last to studio sales.

It is important to assign priorities to particular market channels that hold the most potential. All of the major marketing channels available to you are discussed individually later in the book. As you read about the advantages and disadvantages of each marketing channel you will begin to see that some marketing channels offer greater potential for your particular craft than others. These are the marketing channels that you should use to develop and promote your business. What you will come up with is your own marketing strategy that will get you where you want to be in the least amount of time. Remember that marketing is a creative process and any marketing strategy will change as the marketplace changes. Remember, too, that businesses succeed in spite of falling demand by adapting to satisfy new or different wants and needs.

Chapter 3

Positioning Your Craft

What is positioning? It is a process used to fix a place for a product in a customer's mind. More importantly, it is a way to attract customers in today's advertisement saturated society. It is particularly appropriate for craftsmen and the targeted marketing approach because positioning allows you to focus your message on a specific audience.

Let's look at some facts. The American business community currently spends over $200 per person per year on advertising. If you were to spend $1,000,000 in advertising designed to reach the American public, each person would receive about ½¢ of advertising. Do you think that would have much effect?

Does it make any sense trying to tell everyone in the world about your handmade leather bicycle seats, at great cost and little effect, when you can, for much less money and far greater effect, tell people who already own bicycles about your seats? Positioning lets you identify your audience and present your product to them in such a way that they will buy.

Positioning starts with a product, but it really deals with the way you set that product up in the mind of the consumer. Let's say that you are a fabric designer and you design a fabric with black squares on a red background. You call it Black on Red, and start shipping it to stores all over the country. After a few months you realize that the design has not sold at all! A little research indicates that people are not buying because they want red on black. Your solution? Change the name and call it Red on Black. That's positioning.

Let me give you two examples from the business community. Do you know what the most effective positioning theme was for 7-Up? Sure, the Un-Cola. Why? Because research showed that there were lots of people who did not like cola. Their positioning said, "If you don't like cola, here's the drink for you." Other ad campaigns (positioning themes) for 7-Up have not been nearly as successful. Remember we are talking about exactly the same product, only the positioning is different.

Do you remember Avis? They lost money for years trying to compete with Hertz. They got new management and a new positioning theme: We're Number 2, But We Try Harder. The result? A tremendous increase in sales because people could identify with not being number one and they flocked to give the underdog a chance.

Both of the examples are appropriate to the craft business because 7-Up and Avis are both competing with companies much larger than themselves. Plus, both illustrate a vital positioning principle. Don't fight the other guy! Go over, under or around to find your niche in the marketplace. If you are a potter, it would be insanity to try to produce the same product as Lenox or Corningware. Define what it is they are *not* doing and do that.

☐ WHAT IS IT THAT YOU DO?

Before you can position your product you need to find out what it is that you do. That may sound a little obvious but there are many craftsmen who don't really know, or at least can't define it definitively enough for the marketplace. It is not sufficient to say that you are a weaver, blacksmith, woodworker, potter or jeweler. You need to have a specialty. A blacksmith could specialize in architectural wrought iron work, a woodworker in antique reproductions, a weaver in large-scale commissions, etc., etc.

Successful positioning requires a balance of a unique position and a broad appeal. For any craftsman a broad appeal means enough people interested in your product to insure continued sales. De Lorean positioned his car to appeal to a very limited audience. Rolls Royce has a broader appeal, Mercedes-Benz even broader, and Cadillac the broadest of all, yet all four cars appeal to the affluent audience.

Let's look at a stained glass craftsman and see how he would position his product. Keep in mind that positioning, like any other marketing strategy, is a refining process. The more experience and feedback you get, the better your position will become. Our stained glass craftsman decides that he wants to find his niche in the marketplace. He's attended fairs and galleries and mall shows and knows that there are many people making stained glass. He wants to find an area that nobody is working in, but still has enough demand to keep him employed. He further concludes that he would like to make one-of-a-kind pieces, rather than production work.

☐ LOOK FOR THE HOLE

Our craftsman does some research and discovers a strong demand for stained glass doors and windows in new residential construction. He has found his hole; he is going to design and make stained glass for the new housing market! He makes advice calls on four local builders and finds that he can make door and window inserts at a competitive price and that the builders would be happy to give him the business.

After our craftsman makes a few dozen doors and windows he

finds that he can custom design for individual tastes at little additional cost. So, he gets back in touch with the builders to see if their customers would like such a feature. His idea is received enthusiastically and as the builders offer new home buyers their choice of door and window designs, sales increase and so does the demand for our craftsman's work.

□   TESTING FOR CONSUMER REACTION

Remember that positioning focuses on appealing to the customer. Our glassworker has a good idea that has already proven profitable. He obviously is meeting a need, but how are his customers looking at his work? In other words, why are they really buying? He makes a list of possible reasons:

1. Prompt delivery
2. Competitive price
3. Local businessman
4. Superior product
5. Individual designs

Our craftsman thinks he already knows the answer, but does some additional research and finds that the home salesmen really push the custom design theme because they find that this very often is what is needed to close the deal. A customer feels that the house, not just the doors and windows, is custom designed for him or her. Well, we don't need to carry it any farther. You get the idea. Now that the positioning theme has been tested and proven it's time to:

□   BROADENING THE BASE

Once you have established that you have a quality product at the right price with the right position you can begin to expand your market. That's done by defining additional uses and markets for your craft. Johnson and Johnson broadened its baby shampoo's base by advertising that it was also good for adults. The Florida Orange Growers Association did the same thing with "It's not just for breakfast anymore." You can do the same thing by naturally expanding your market after you have established a position.

□   YOUR POSITIONING THEME

A positioning theme is like a road map. You know where you are, where you want to be and have a plan for getting there. And that is far better than running around in 100 different directions hoping to find something. A position statement isn't forever. Look at banks five years ago and compare them with today's "Financial Advisory Centers." And did you ever wonder what happened to the neighborhood gas station? Today they are all self-service mini-marts.

Take whatever time you need right now to define your own positioning theme. Here are some areas to consider:

1. What is your product?
2. Who is your competition and what are they doing?
3. What's the hole?
4. What is your target audience?
5. What is your positioning theme?
6. What marketing channels will you use?

This is not intended to be the final solution. As you read more and test more, you'll be able to refine your position. All we want here is a beginning.

Chapter 4

Planning for Profit

Okay. You know what you want to do and have a plan for doing it. Any marketing strategy should be well thought out, well researched and *implemented only if all the data indicates that it will be profitable.* You may have the best product in the world, but if nobody will buy it at a price that allows you a profit, you cannot stay in the crafts business. Product profit potential is researched in two stages: determining profit potential in the general marketplace and determining profitability in specific marketing channels.

Any item you produce competes with other items in the marketplace. In other words, your business will be fighting with other businesses for your share of the consumer dollar. In order to effectively compare your sales with others, you need to be using the same measurements and terms. Here's a review of some of the basic selling terms used in business.

□ SALES TERMINOLOGY

Selling Costs
What is actually costs you to make a sale. Let's say that you have prepared a direct mail package for galleries and shops. The total cost of the mailer (including postage) is $2.00. You send out 100 and 10% of the galleries respond with orders. Your actual selling cost in this instance is $20 per customer but it may be well worth it because many of the customers will be repeat customers and will order again and again.

Selling costs are relative. I know one company that estimates that it spends $200 to locate and qualify prospective customers for its sales staff. The company feels that it's getting a good deal because its sales staff closes 33% of the customers they talk with and after paying the salesman's commission the company still receives a gross profit of $2500.

Gross Profit
The amount you receive before deducting any expenses. If you own a gallery and sell another craftsman's work for $10, and you bought it at the wholesale price of $5, you have realized a gross profit of $5.

Net Profits
The amount you have remaining after deducting operating expenses. Using the same gallery example, your net profit would be less because you would need to deduct the expense of operating the gallery.

Indirect Costs
Costs of doing business other than the actual cost of the object or materials. Insurance, rent, heat, taxes, etc., etc., are considered indirect costs.

Direct Costs
The cost of the item you are selling. If you are selling from the same gallery and the wholesale price of a mug is $3.00 and it retails for $6.00, your direct cost is $3.00.

Credit
Offering credit is a necessity in today's market, particularly if you are selling to other businesses. We are concerned here with short-term credit, the kind that you offer for 30 days at no interest. In establishing credit for commercial customers you must decide:

1. Whom you should grant credit to
2. How much credit to allow
3. What your terms and collection policies are
4. When to terminate credit

Many craftspeople make it a policy never to grant credit to a customer until he has established an account and has paid for his first order in advance.

Credit Cards
These are also known as bank cards. These have become such a prevalent part of our economy that you will lose sales if you do not accept credit cards for purchases. Research has shown that allowing your customers to use their MasterCard, Visa or American Express cards to purchase crafts from you substantially increases sales. In marketing terminology, this is known as an exchange function because you are making it easier to own your craft item by making it easier for the customer to pay.

It is a fairly easy matter to set up a charge card service with your local bank. There will be a fee to process your application and you should expect to provide financial information on your business and to undergo a routine credit check. Once your application has been approved there will be a fee of about $30 for the imprinter and a one-time set-up fee of about $35. After that there is a service charge ranging for 2% to 7% on all transactions to your account. The rate varies according to the volume of sales you record each month.

Credit cards also come in handy for your own personal or business use. These can be especially valuable when you are out of town or are making a purchase by phone. Many craftspeople use charge cards for all their expenses away from home because the bills are sent to their business and provide a clear and concise record of all their business-related expenses.

Terms

There are a variety of payment terms that you can agree upon with your customers. Here are the standard ones:

Net 30 Days is the most common payment term and simply means that the customer must pay the invoice within thirty days.

2% 10 Days Net 30 Days rewards the customer for prompt payment by giving him a 2% discount if he pays within 10 days, otherwise the full amount is due in 30 days.

3% 10 E.O.M. is sometimes used with larger accounts such as department stores. It allows the buyer a month and 10 days to pay the account and allows the buyer a 3% discount if he pays within this time frame. High volume stores may request an even higher discount rate, but the theory is the same: the cheaper they can buy your crafts and the longer they can take to pay, the more profit they make.

10 Days Net is what you should specify if you want or need prompt payment.

C.O.D. is another way of collecting your money. C.O.D. stands for cash on delivery, and means that your order will not be delivered to your customer until the delivery agent collects the full value.

Shipping Costs

The price of sending goods is always paid by the person ordering the goods. If in doubt, note on your invoices that all orders are shipped F.O.B. (the location of your studio). My invoice reads: All Orders Shipped F.O.B. Stone Mountain, GA 30083.

Claims

What happens if your order arrives at its destination partially broken? Who's responsible for the damages, you or the buyer? Well, it's the responsibility of the shipping company, but someone has to make the claim and in almost every instance it is the receiver of the goods who is responsible for initiating the claim, because he can certify that the goods are damaged. A good policy is to deduct the amount of the loss due to damage from the customer's bill after you have received a copy of the damage claim. It is then your responsibility to collect the damages. It means extra effort for you, but it's great for business relations.

Returns

Returns are rare. Craftspeople care about their work and almost always are careful about quality control and packing. However, customers do return things every once in a while and you should refund their money if they have a legitimate excuse and if return it within a reasonable length of time.

Minimum Order

Set a limit on how small an order you will accept. One hundred dollars seems to be the standard minimum order, but you can establish what is best for you. Don't fool around with $10 orders from 100 different people in 100 different locations.

Sample Order

Agree to ship sample orders for first-time customers. Shop and gallery owners like to be able to test the market before they buy in volume. Send a sample order when requested, but insist on minimum order/re-orders.

Exclusive Rights

Some shops will ask for an exclusive right to sell your work in their particular geographical area. Sometimes it is in your best interest, sometimes it is not. If it is a quality shop in a rural area or in another state, you probably would be safe in granting an exclusive. If, however, a shop in your hometown wants an exclusive and there are ten other shops selling crafts of equal quality, I'd think twice about getting tied down with an exclusive.

Cash Flow

Every single business is likely to find itself short of cash occasionally, especially when it's growing and sales outrun payments. In business, a good account pays in 30 days, but some wait 60 or 90 days. Your problem, particularly as a new business owner, is many of your suppliers want cash up-front. You will need some cash reserve to assure yourself that you have enough money to pay your bills while you are waiting for your customers to pay the bills they owe you.

When you don't have enough money in your checking account to pay your bills, you have a cash flow problem. Accountants call it 'lack of liquidity' or a need for more 'working capital.' What can you do yourself that you have enough money to pay your bills while you are waiting for your customers to pay the bills they owe you.

When you don't have enough money in your checking account to pay your bills, you have a cash flow problem. Accountants call it 'lack of liquidity' or a need for more 'working capital.' What can you do about it? There are several steps to take:

1. Have a cash reserve on hand to get through the rough spots.
2. Try to get your customers to pay faster by offering them a discount for prompt payment. (2% net 10 days is one possibility)

3. See if suppliers will give you terms on your payments to them.
4. Stagger your payments to your creditors. If company A bills on the 10th and company B on the 20th and each gives a discount on bills paid within 10 days, pay A on the 20th and B on the 30th. You get free use of their money for 10 extra days.

Speaking the language of business is one step. The next step is to determine whether you can compete in the marketplace.

□ ARE YOUR PRICES COMPETITIVE?

The first step in determining overall market competition is to do a survey of what similar products are selling for. Keep it simple at this stage. Don't be concerned about who made it or what market channel it's being sold in. What you want to determine is the average sales price for a product similar to the one you are making.

Let's take wooden toys as an example. If you make a small wooden car and your research indicates that the average retail price for the same size and quality car is $6, that is your market price. Wait! Before you start saying, "Yes, but . . . ," I already know all the "Yes, buts." I know that you can build a reputation and charge more for your product and I know that the same product can sell for more or less depending on the market channel. You'll have a chance to individualize your price according to market channel later. Right now we need to keep it simple.

Your research should answer one question: Can you produce an equal product at the current retail selling price and make a profit? If you can't, don't. I recommend that you spend some additional time researching why you can't make if for the average selling price, but if the answer is still no, drop that idea and go on to another. Keep in mind that most new product ideas never make it to the marketplace, so it's better to find out in the initial stages than after you have invested thousands of dollars.

How do you find out if you can make an item at a profit, assuming you sell it at the current retail price? You first figure out what it costs you to make the item, using the formula: Direct Costs plus Indirect Costs plus Labor equal Production Cost. Again, the wooden toy car is used as an example.

Computing Direct Costs
Begin by listing all the materials used to produce the car:

Wood	21¢
Wheels (4)	20¢
Dowels (for axles)	10¢
Sandpaper	2¢
String	6¢
Varnish	1¢
Total	60¢

The additional costs all come under the heading of overhead, or indirect costs, and include such things as: electricity, heat, office expenses, rent, advertising, travel, etc., etc., and they can really add up.

Indirect Costs
A sample listing of the overhead expenses for a year might look like this:

Utilities	$ 1,200
Mortgage	5,400
Office Supplies	300
Advertising	2,000
Insurance	500
Taxes	2,800
Depreciation	1,200
Professional Services	450
Transportation	1,100
Meals away from home	1,200
Postage	300
Lodging	1,000
Misc.	250
Total	$17,700

Computing Labor Costs
The next step is to add labor costs to indirect costs to determine total operating costs per year.

Let's assume that our toymaker works 2,000 hours a year (40 hours per week for 50 weeks). His annual salary is $20,000, so his hourly wage is $10.

Adding the yearly indirect costs ($17,700) and the annual salary ($20,000), we get a yearly operating expense of $37,700. Dividing that by the number of hours worked, we see that it is costing our toymaker $18.85 an hour to stay in business. He can make 9 cars an hour, so each car is costing him $2.10 in operating costs. (In actuality, our toymaker can complete 12 cars an hour, but he knows from his records that ¼ of his studio time is devoted to non-production activities, such as packing buying supplies, etc. He, therefore, multiplies his actual hourly production by .75 to get a more realistic production count.) If we add material costs of $.60 per car, we get a total production cost of $2.70 per car.

Our goal here is determining market profitability. Based on the analysis of the wooden car's production cost of $2.70 and a retail sales price of $6, the indication would be that this is a profitable item, at least in the retail market (remember that selling costs have not been computed yet). Obviously, this is a simplified version because you need to do a cost analysis of each item in your inventory to determine the profitability of your product line. But the process is the same as used in the car example.

What happens if some or all of your items are so expensive to make that you cannot sell them at the going rate and still make a profit? You have two choices: either don't make those items or reduce your production costs so that the items will be competitive and profitable. You may by able to buy your materials at a more reasonable costs, or increase your production efficiency or lower your indirect costs, or, or, or . . . .

You'll be able to figure that all out for yourself. Just be honest with the figures you use. It doesn't matter how long you have been a craftsman, you should always do a market price analysis for each new product you develop. I'll talk later about individualized prices for specific market channels, but you should know before you start production of any item whether or not it can compete effectively in the marketplace.

Chapter 5

Determining Market Channel Profitability

In the last chapter we determined overall market profitability for a single item. The assumption is made here that you have conducted an analysis of the marketplace profitability for all the items you make and have retained only those craft items that can profitably compete. Now you need more information because like any good business owner you want to know:

1. Which of your products sell best.
2. Which products sell best in each market channel.
3. Which market channel is the most efficient.
4. Which marketing channels are most profitable.
5. Which items you make the most profit on.

The first step in seeking answers to our important questions is to take stock of what we have on hand for inventory. There really is no magic to this: it's simply a record of what you have made, where it was sold, and how many you have left. I prefer using a separate inventory sheet for each item. Let's return to our toymaker again and see what a typical inventory sheet might look like.

PRODUCT IDENTIFICATION   CAR

Date	Transaction	Produced	Sold	Remaining
1/4/84	Rainblue Gallery		10	23
1/8/84	Production	20		43
1/12/84	Studio Sales		4	39
1/23/84	Craft Show (Yellow Daisy)		12	27
2/2/84	Studio Sales		2	25
2/4/84	Mail-Order		2	23
2/19/84	Children's Playland		10	13
3/5/84	Classic Toys		12	1
	Total		62	

Type up your own version of the inventory sheet and take it to a local printer to have a few hundred copies run off. It will only cost a few dollars but you will have them handy when you need them. A convenient size for inventory sheets is the standard size 8½ by 11 inch paper.

Note that there is a section to record the type of transaction. This is essential because later you will want to know what type of market channel is working best for you and your inventory sheets will tell you because you have identified the market channel on your inventory sheet.

If our toymaker wants to know what items sold best at craft fairs during the last three months, he could refer to the inventory sheets and record all the sales for crafts fairs for each item. All of these figures are then entered onto a Quarterly Sales Analysis Form which gives you a summary of your quarterly volume for each item and each marketing area. Our toymaker's analysis may look something like this ——————→

The Quarterly Sales Analysis for January, February and March shows that the best seller for the period was the car with 244 sales; the worst seller was the key rack with 34 sales. The sales at department stores and mall shows (236 and 234, respectively) were the highest and the sales at the craft fairs the lowest.

It's a simple matter to combine the four quarterly sales sheets into one, making it a Yearly Sales Analysis. Why bother with the Quarterly Sales Analysis in the first place? Because they give you additional information about trends. Some craftsmen use monthly sales analysis forms for even greater sales predictability.

Looking at the Yearly Sales Analysis sheet, we see that the top selling item for the year was the car, with the key rack again coming in last. It is also clear that mall shows, department stores and mail order accounted for the highest volume of sales.

So, using a simple record keeping system, you can determine what the sales are for each craft item you make and can determine what market channels are responsible for the highest sales volume.

But we still don't have enough information. It's important to know:

1. Which marketing channel is most efficient.
2. Which marketing channel is the most profitable.
3. Which products are the most profitable.

No, we haven't already answered those questions. We know which products and which markets account for the most sales, but that doesn't necessarily mean that they are the most efficient or profitable. Let's take our questions one at a time.

QUARTERLY SALES ANALYSIS

Craft Items

Months Jan., Feb., March

Year 1984

	Car	Boat	Sailboat	Bus	Truck	Train	Train & Cars	Duck	Dog	Mouse	Cat	Windvane	Key Rack	Hat Rack	Small Bird	Large Bird	Airplane	Dump Truck	Total
Craft Fairs	24	4	10	4	12	2	4	20	2	0	0	8	4	2	2	2	8	4	112
Shops/Galleries	48	12	10	8	12	12	0	24	12	2	4	20	2	16	4	6	16	2	210
In-Shop Sales	32	2	16	4	14	4	24	2	2	10	16	8	2	16	8	4	14	16	194
Mall Shows	96	24	20	4	4	2	10	8	12	14	4	4	2	6	18	20	22	12	282
Mail Order	20	16	24	2	2	6	8	6	6	16	8	8	8	16	24	22	28	14	234
Dept. Store	24	8	24	16	16	12	8	4	2	18	12	12	16	24	4	14	24	2	236
Total	244	86	104	38	60	38	54	64	36	60	44	60	34	80	60	68	112	50	

YEARLY SALES ANALYSIS

YEAR 1984

	Car	Boat	Sailboat	Bus	Truck	Train	Train & Cars	Duck	Dog	Mouse	Cat	Windvane	Key Rack	Hat Rack	Small Bird	Large Bird	Airplane	Dump Truck	Total
Craft Fairs	96	16	40	16	48	8	16	80	8	0	0	32	16	8	8	8	32	16	448
Shops/Galleries	192	48	40	32	48	48	0	96	48	8	16	80	8	64	16	24	64	8	840
In-Shop Sales	128	8	64	16	56	16	96	8	8	40	64	32	8	64	32	16	56	64	776
Mall Shows	384	96	80	16	16	8	40	32	48	56	16	16	8	24	73	80	88	48	1128
Mail Order	80	64	96	8	8	24	32	24	32	64	32	32	32	64	96	88	112	56	936
Department Store	96	32	96	64	64	48	32	16	8	72	48	48	64	96	16	56	96	8	944
Total	976	344	416	152	240	152	216	256	144	240	176	240	136	320	240	272	448	200	

□   MARKET EFFICIENCY

After you have made a craft item, how much effort does it take to sell it? That's what market efficiency is concerned with: sales ratio to effort. Our toymaker may have exhibited at 10 different mall shows to sell the volume he did, but could have sold all his toys to one department store to account for his sales in that market channel. Sales costs at the mall show may be high, but he will be selling at retail price. Selling costs to the department store may be much less, but he will be selling at wholesale price.

Our toymaker is selling the same product at the mall show that he sells at the department store, so his actual manufacturing costs are the same. But how much sales time does he need to sell at a mall show and how much to sell to a department store? Remember that there are only so many hours in a day so that sales time takes away from production time.

Our toymaker exhibited at 10 different mall shows last year and for each; he recorded the time it took to pack up, drive to the show, put up his display, staff the booth, take down the display, drive home and unpack. He added the time up for each show and got a total for all 10 shows of 320 hours (32 hours for each show). He then divided the number of items sold (1128) into the number of hours required to sell them and came up with a time of 17 minutes. That's the amount of time it takes to sell each item at a mall show.

The toymaker takes his samples to four different department store buyers, one of whom buys. She buys for a chain of stores and when she sees the initial order selling well, she orders more, accounting for the toymaker's total sales of 944. Adding the time for the four interviews, follow-up phone calls, packing and transportation, we have a total of 12 hours. The sales time divided by the total number of items sold (944) gives us a sales time per item of less than one minute.

What does this mean? It means that wholesaling to department stores is 17 times more efficient than selling at mall shows. It means that for every toy our craftsman produces in his studio, he will have to spend 17 more minutes selling it at a mall show. In an hour he can sell over 60 toys to the department store, less than four at a mall show. At an hourly wage of $10, it would cost him 16¢ each to sell to a department store and $2.83 to sell at the mall show.

Okay, we see that in this particular comparison of just two marketing channels that one is significantly more efficient than another. Using the same formula (total sales time divided by number of items sold) you can easily determine the sales efficiency of any marketing channel.

□   MARKET CHANNEL PROFIT PROFILE

The next step is to determine which market channel is the most profitable. At first glance looking at our Yearly Sales Analysis, we would conclude that the mall show was the most profitable channel because more items were sold in that channel, but that may not be the case when all the figures are analyzed.

Before we begin our analysis, we must agree that actual production costs do not vary from channel to channel. The two variables that do determine market channel profitability are selling price and selling cost.

Returning to our toymaker once again, we look at two market channels, the mall show and the department store. For the purposes of illustration let's say that the average production cost for all the toys is $4.50 each, including materials, overhead and labor, and let's further say that the average retail selling price for all the toys is an average of $10.00. Here's how our two market channels would compare:

The Mall Show		Department Stores	
Sales Price	$10.00	Sales Price	$ 5.00
Less Production Cost	$ 4.50	Less Production Costs	$ 4.50
Less Sales Cost	$ 2.83	Less Sales Cost	$ .16
Profit	$ 2.87	Profit	$ .34

It is obvious that the mall show is the more profitable channel. Take the time to compute your own market channel profitability using this formula: Sales Price minus Manufacturing Cost minus Sales Cost equals Profit. The results may surprise you, but at least you will be aware of which market channels offer the highest and lowest profits, plus all those in between.

This information will help you formulate your targeted marketing system which means (at this stage, anyway) that you'll have a good idea of where you want to concentrate your marketing efforts.

☐ ITEM PROFITABILITY

Knowing which market channels offer the greatest profit margin is extremely helpful. Now we are ready to determine the profitability of each item you make in each market channel. This will allow you to concentrate your marketing efforts on the most profitable items in the most profitable market channels. Why sell refrigerators in Alaska when you can sell condominiums in Florida?

We'll take the toy car again as our example. The chart below indicates the profit for the car in each market channel.

	sales price	man. costs	sales costs	profit
Craft Fairs	$6.00	$2.70	$2.75	$ .55
Galleries	$3.00	$2.70	$ .20	$ .10
Studio Sales	$6.00	$2.70	$ .10	$3.20
Mall Shows	$6.00	$2.70	$2.83	$ .47
Mail Order	$6.00	$2.70	$3.00	$ .30
Department Stores	$3.00	$2.70	$ .16	$ .14

It is a simple matter to determine profitability for each item in your inventory by following the procedure as above. In the example the price for the car was the same for each market channel. The only difference in price was determined by wholesale and retail selling markets.

However, in your analysis you may find that the same item may sell for different prices depending on the market. For example, you may find that a particular type of leather belt sells best for $10 at a fair, but sells best at $12 through mail order. Use these figures to determine the true profitability of each item in each market channel.

Remember that each market channel has its own unique characteristics and a specific marketing plan needs to be developed for each one. That includes individualized pricing and long range profitability.

Individualized Pricing

Market competition will often set price limits, but the prices your competition charges are based on consumer acceptance and perception. Did you know that a Cadillac costs only a few hundred dollars more to produce than a comparably equipped Chevrolet? But what is the difference in selling price? Thousands of dollars! And why are consumers willing to pay thousands of dollars more for the same basic automobile? Perception! The Cadillac looks more luxurious, the showrooms are more impressive, the salespeople give more personal service, etc., etc.

What this all comes down to is that you should charge what the customer wants to pay. Companies not only test market for consumer reaction to a new product, they test market for consumer reaction to price. For example, mail order businesses will advertise the same product at three different prices in three different magazines. The price that gets the most people to buy and, therefore, brings in the greatest profit, is the price used for the larger follow-up advertisements. If twice as many people will buy your hand-printed fabric at $20 a yard than people will at $15 a yard, wouldn't you be foolish to charge $15 even though you can make a profit at that price?

Test market your prices. All you really need to keep in mind is the minimum price you need to charge. If the consumer perceives your product as being worth more and is willing to pay more, then that is the price you should charge.

Long Range Profitability

Some market channels show low initial profitability, but will bring in higher profits down the line. The classic example of this is mail order. Initial costs for each customer are high; all successful mail order businesses expect to break even or even lose money on initial orders. It is the back-end or follow-up sales where mail order businesses make their profits. So, in our example of the toymaker, the profit on mail order was low, but follow-up sales will change the eventual profit picture.

☐   SUMMARY

Returning to the five questions posed at the beginning of the chapter we conclude:

1. Which products sell best? Obviously, the car in our example, followed by the airplane, sailboat, and motor boat. The others seem to sell about the same with the exception of the bus, train, dog and key rack which sell poorly, suggesting they might need to be redesigned or replaced.

2. Which products sell best in each marketing channel? The yearly sales analysis shows that the car sells best at mall shows, the sailboat has the greatest sales in mail order, etc., etc. Using this information, you can develop a priority marketing profile for each market channel. For example, in the craft fair channel, the best seller is the car, then the duck, the sailboat, the windvane and the airplane, etc., etc. Simply by listing your items in order of sales for each market channel, you have a market sales profile for each area.

3. Which market channels are most profitable? In our example, the studio sales were the most profitable followed by fairs, mall shows, mail order, department stores and galleries. However, we realize that in-studio sales will not generate the volume of sales needed, so a marketing strategy must be developed using other marketing channels.

4. Which market channel is the most efficient? Generally, wholesale markets are more efficient because they take care of the selling. In our example, the department store was more efficient than the mall show, but further research would probably have indicated that gallery and wholesale show sales would have been as efficient.

5. Which items are the most profitable? This is more difficult to answer because the same item can sell for different prices in different market channels. If we take the car again with a production cost of $2.70 and a sales price of $6.00, we get a per item profit of $3.30 from which we must deduct any sales cost. Using the same procedure you can easily determine the per item profitability in each market channel. The ideal is to sell your highest profit items in the highest profit market channel. For example, if the car and the airplane were the two highest profit items it would make sense to have them prominently displayed in your studio, the highest profit market channel.

A targeted marketing approach uses market research to formulate a profit plan. Our toymaker now knows what is selling in what market channel and at what profit. Can he take advantage of that? Sure! He knows that studio sales offer him the highest profit so he may open his shop on weekends, advertise with the state tourist bureau, relocate his studio to a more heavily traveled highway, or invite customers to special seasonal sales at his studio. Long range plans may call for keeping his shop open six days a week, so he may consider mail order as a secondary market because it has high volume potential and will allow him to sell without leaving his studio.

Nobody can tell you what your specific marketing plan will be. You'll need to work that out for yourself. But at least you know how and will have some facts to base your marketing strategy on. Remember that marketing is constantly changing in response to customers' wants and needs. Keep analyzing your products and keep monitoring their performance for best results.

Chapter 6

Keeping in Touch with Your Market

There are three essential ingredients in maintaining any successful marketing plan.

1. Keeping track of market trends
2. Servicing current and future accounts
3. Developing and testing new products

It does not matter how accurately you position your product and how successful you are in building your business, if you fail to continue to meet the consumers' needs, your business will fall off and possibly fail.

It is appropriate here to say that nobody has all the answers in marketing. People are successful in business because they maximize their winners and minimize their losers. In other words, by paying attention to the three ingredients of continuing market planning, a craftsman can achieve marketing success.

□ PREDICTING MARKET TRENDS

The one thing that is constant in life is change and that is certainly true of the craft market. The theory of trend prediction is based on the fact that things do change and they change at predictable rates. There will be certain instances when changes do not occur as predicted, but in the long run, there is a predictable pattern that occurs and you can use this pattern to anticipate changes in demand for your craft products. The ability to predict with some accuracy will allow you to keep your business healthy in spite of changes in consumer demand.

Trend prediction is based on the fact that any product goes through three stages:

1. The developmental and testing stage
2. The buyer acceptance stage
3. The buyer rejection stage

In graph form, it looks like a flat mountain.

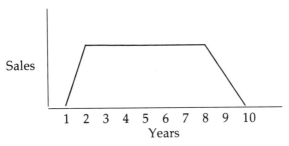

The Developmental and Testing Stage

The base of the mountain on the left indicates The Developmental and Testing Stage. This is where the product is made in small numbers and tested for consumer reaction. If initial response indicates that the product should be tested further, more models are made and a larger population used to test market. If these results are still positive the item gets a green light and is put into full scale production with a matching advertising effort. As the product is introduced to the public, sales climb at a rather rapid rate until it reaches its given percentage of the market. It is then at:

The Acceptance Stage

This is where the product will stay unless some unforeseen event significantly changes the public's perception of that product. The Tylenol poisonings is one such example of such an unforeseen event. What does this mean to you? It means that for almost every product you develop there will be a time needed to introduce it to the public after which it will reach a certain sales level where it will remain for some time. When sales begin to drop, the product is most likely entering:

The Buyer Rejection Stage

When demand for your product falls, it is probably not due to any fault of yours, but is most likely due to changing consumer tastes. When you begin to see a decline in sales, it is time to begin to think about phasing that product out and developing a new one to take its place.

You may decide that your current production of twenty different craft items is all the variety you can handle. That's fine, but you should anticipate that the actual selection of items will be changing as marketing demands change. That means that the twenty craft items you will produce five years from now will not be exactly the same twenty you are producing today.

You can see from the graph that the downward trend often is rather dramatic after it begins. If you keep careful track of quarterly trends, you will be able to see patterns developing and will be able to change your production and marketing plans accordingly.

It doesn't matter how hard you've worked and how success-fully you have tracked your profit and losses and responded to chang-ing market conditions, you will still have a struggle unless you develop a method of:

□   KEEPING TRACK OF CURRENT AND FUTURE
    ACCOUNTS

Everyone's heard of the old saying, "A bird in the hand is worth two in the bush." Let me apply that to craft marketing and para-phrase by saying: "An established customer is worth ten potential cus-tomers." Why? Because an established customer, who has purchased your work, has demonstrated that you have met at least one of his wants and as long as you continue to meet his wants, he will continue to be a customer. Allow me to reinforce this point by using an example from mail order marketing. A 2% response from a direct mail campaign is considered good, which means that if you send out letters about your craft products to 100 potential customers you will get two people who will buy, if you're lucky. In this case, a customer in the hand is worth fifty in the mail box.

Remember that selling crafts is a personal business, so when you have established a customer, do everything you can to convey that you care about him or her personally. This almost happens automat-ically when you deal with shops and galleries because most of them are run by the owners, but you should insist on the same personal contact when you establish accounts with larger volume dealers, such as department stores and mail order businesses.

Make a folder for each of your commercial accounts. Inside, file a copy of all the orders sent to that account so that you know what they have ordered. Inside the folder, staple to the left side, a personal note sheet. It should include the name and address of the business, who the owner is, a business phone number and room for notes. Have the folder in front of you every time you call that particular account.

Whenever you contact your accounts it's easy to use the per-sonal data sheet to make an individualized, no-pressure sales pitch, such as: "Bob? This is Brian Jefferson. How is your family? . . . You remember the last time we talked you mentioned that you had had numerous requests for salt and pepper shakers and were unable to get any? I've been thinking about that and have reproduced some samples in three different designs that I thought you'd like to try. Naturally, I'll take them back if they don't sell, but if they do, you and I could both make a little more money. I've also got a good inventory on hand right now, so if you are getting low on any items, now might be a good time to restock. I can jot down what you need over the phone and get it out to you in a couple of days."

I highly recommend the personal approach. It makes a great difference in sales, and I know it works because salesmen have been using the same technique for years. Several years ago, I went to a qual-ity clothing store and bought a sports jacket. The salesman was most helpful and gave me his card. For some reason, I held on to the card and gave him a call when I was ready to make another purchase. When I arrived, he remembered my name, size, the members of my family, where I worked, etc., etc. To put it mildly, I was impressed. So I asked him how he remembered all that. He said, "Oh, that's easy! Right after I served you last time, I wrote up a card on you because I sort of figured that you would be back and I wanted to be able to serve you even better than the last time!" He profits because he gets a commission on each purchase I make from him, and I profit because I get excellent service at not extra cost to me.

And if that isn't enough reason to keep track of your accounts, there is another one: established accounts greatly reduce selling costs. As an example, let's refer back to our direct mail campaign. Suppose the flyer you sent out about your work cost 30¢ each, plus 20¢ postage, for a total cost of 50¢ per mailed piece. One hundred letters cost $50 and with a 2% response, you have a selling cost of $25 for each customer. This may well be worth it in the long run because the likelihood is that a customer will reorder if satisfied. However, keep in mind that once your customer list is established it only costs you 50¢ to stay in touch — a very effective use of your advertising dollar.

☐ DEVELOPING NEW PRODUCTS

Small business is in! You have a tremendous advantage over big business in new product development because you can create and test market a new product almost overnight without any fear of major expense or effort on your part. Chrysler took an 800,000,000 dollar gamble with its K car and, fortunately, won, enabling them to pay off their government loans early. Other gambles have not worked so well. Remember the Edsel and the Corvair?

If you want to test new designs, something you should be doing constantly anyway, all you need to do is make up a few samples and try them in the markets you are currently using. If the response is good, you can expand your test marketing to determine the best price, packaging, and markets. If the response is not good, determine why not. If it's a design that the customers just don't want, it's best to find out early so that you can minimize your losses and concentrate on producing designs that are responsive to the market.

Keeping in mind your production capacity, your goal should be to produce the fastest selling, most profitable items in your inventory. When items begin to drop in sales, be ready to phase them out in favor of new items. When an old item is in the buyer rejection stage, you should have several items already in the development and testing stage ready to take its place.

You'll constantly be getting clues about consumer wants for new items through your contacts with them. Listen to the marketplace and respond to consumer demand. Your continued success depends on it.

PART TWO

Retail Marketing
Methods

Chapter 7

Retail Marketing Strategies

Selling crafts at retail is by far the largest crafts marketing channel. It is estimated that sales at craft fairs alone top a third of a billion dollars a year and when you add in sales at mall shows and sales directly from the studio you are talking about a lot of money.

□ ADVANTAGES

There are two principal advantages; you sell at retail price, thus getting more money for each item you sell and secondly, because you are selling directly to the customer in a face-to-face situation you can keep track of market demands. I'll elaborate on these two advantages and list some others as well, but let's talk about the two main advantages in more detail first.

When you retail your work you really are acting as your own agent. You wear many hats because you manufacture, advertise, display, deliver and sell your product. The advantage is that you know your product intimately and can probably sell it more effectively than anyone else. The reward is that you get what your manufacturing costs are plus you get the margin a retailer receives by selling it for you.

Working with customers in a face-to-face situation allows you to stay in touch with market demands. When someone stops by your display the questions he or she asks could very well lead to additional ideas and additional sales. If your work is all done in browns and every other person you talk to likes your work but wants it in blue, you have the kind of direct market feed-back that is vital to your success. By the way, large companies pay thousands and even millions of dollars for the same direct market analysis. Remember, it is not how *you* perceive your product but how *your* customer perceives it that makes the difference.

Another advantage of direct retail selling, particularly in the craft and mall show channels, is that you can see what the competition is doing. I don't know about you but I readily admit that every craft item I produce is not totally my original idea. I have learned from others and have adapted some of their ideas to my own way of working.

Others have done exactly the same thing and you should too.

Direct sales also lets you get names and addresses of your customers for future sales. Don't overlook this aspect of your business. Have them sign your guest book or sign up for your mailing list. I know a potter who uses a very effective technique. When someone buys one of his pots he makes out a registration card with the description of the item and the customer's name and address. He then tells his customer, "I'll keep this on file. If you would ever like another or if for some reason the one you just bought is broken or lost, I'll be able to replace it for you." The customers love the personal attention and of course receive mailings of new shows and new items.

One craftsman moved from Florida to New Jersey and because she had kept track of all her customers at her Florida studio, was able to develop a profitable mail-order business with them even though she was 1200 miles away.

□ DISADVANTAGES

All of us learn quickly that everything has a good side and a bad side. While it's true that you can make a lot of money in the stock market it is also true that you can loose as well. The two principal disadvantages of retail selling: It takes a lot of time, time that you could use in the studio producing; and selling costs are much higher than in the wholesale market.

Retail marketing requires that you do everything, including selling. That means that you must pack up your items, travel to the fair or show, set up your display and man the booth for the duration of the show. Sales from your studio require less effort, but you still must size up your customers. Some customers love to come in and talk for hours but buy nothing. Some craftsmen have threatened to charge chatty but non-buying customers by the hour.

Selling costs are high and in some cases consume any profit. Earlier we saw how to figure production and sales costs. Whatever time you spend away from the studio is non-productive and must be figured carefully into costs. For example, if you don't sell enough at retail to make up for the time away from the studio then you would make more money selling at wholesale and having more time in your studio to make crafts. If the customers who stop by your studio take up so much of your time that your production is limited then you'll have to consider another selling strategy.

Don't forget to figure in traveling expenses, entry fees, sales taxes and other items that all add to selling costs. Even when you sell from the studio, you have reduced the size of your work space in order to have space to effectively display your work. If you had all the space for work could you produce more items? If the answer is yes then the display area in your studio is costing you money and must be figured into the total selling costs.

□ PRESENTING YOUR WORK

In any retail market the presentation of your work plays a large part in making sales. The customer must have an initial good impression to sell to him. Obviously, not everyone who stops at your display will buy but nobody will buy if they are so turned off by the initial impression that they don't want to investigate further.

You face two types of juries; those who judge the suitability of your work for inclusion in their craft fair or mall show, and the individual jury — the customer. Both are equally important, but in the case of the craft show you have to get by a jury of your peers before you get a chance to be judged by your customers.

Craft fair and mall show promoters are in the business to make money. In order to do so they must put together a show that attracts enough craftsmen to fill all the booths, each paying a fee for the privilege of exhibiting. The promoter must also attract enough customers so that the exhibitors have sufficient sales to want to exhibit the following year. Putting this all together is not always an easy task. So when looking at your work and the work of other craftsmen who have applied, the show manager and the show jury will try to get the right mix of quality and variety that will induce customers to come and buy.

Because every show is different, the crafts selected are different. Many craftsmen believe that the only reason for rejection is the quality of the work. That is not always the case. Sometimes work will be rejected because it is too good or is not the type of work that the typical customer attending that show is interested in. The frustrating thing is that seldom do juries give any reason for rejection or acceptance; you're just in or out.

What do you do then? Well, later I'll describe some specific techniques that you can use. For now, just keep in mind that each show is looking for a particular kind of work. If you take the time to do a little research to learn what a particular show is like, your chances of selecting and being accepted into the right show increases dramatically.

If you are concentrating on selling from your studio you won't have to deal with a preliminary jury, only the final one, the customer. If the customer is the final jury it is tempting to conclude "if it sells, it's good." But that's not the final solution by any means. The craftsman must always balance his own integrity with the demands of the market. If he produces only what the market wants then he has given up his responsibility to educate the consumer as to the uniqueness and quality of his work.

My recommendation is to take the time to define what it is that you do and then find jurors who respect your work. You'll feel better about what you are doing and the higher quality of your work will permit you to demand higher prices.

☐ HOW TO SELECT THE RIGHT AMOUNT OF INVENTORY

The cardinal rule to be kept in mind, always, is that the customer must be able to choose from a selection of items. This holds true whether you are showing at a crafts fair or selling from your studio. It means that the display must always look like it is freshly stocked and offers the customer a wide choice of your finest work.

Some craftsmen make the mistake of planning for a certain number of sales and bringing just that quantity to the show. The result is that the booth, after the first day looks bare and people feel that all the best stuff has already been sold. So they move on to other booths that offer them a full selection to choose from.

When you have been in business for a while you will have some statistics on what sold in previous years. You can use the figures to determine what you need this year. If you are entering a market for the first time bring more than you think you will need. Sure, you'll have some left over but your sales will be better than if you had not stocked enough.

Use a similar approach in selling from your studio. The customer always wants a selection. Keep your display area well stocked with samples of everything you make. Don't display every single item you have in stock, just samples of each so that the customer can see what's available.

☐ SELECTING THE RIGHT ITEMS

One of the most frequently asked questions is "How do I know which items will sell?" The answer is you don't, particularly if you are doing the show for the first time. You have to make an educated guess based on your research. After that it will be a refining process in which you plan ahead to bring those items that sold well before, plus some new items to test market.

Some craftsmen divide their work into production and one-of-a-kind, or functional and ornamental. If it helps to use these categories go ahead and use them. I sometimes find it difficult to define which is which. I believe it is more effective to keep track of sales and use proven winners as the basis of your selection.

Product Suitability

If your product is well made and realistically priced there is a market for it. However, it is sometimes difficult determining what that market is. Many, many craftspeople have lost potential sales because they gave up too quickly. They tried one or two shows and were disappointed with the sales so stopped going to shows.

Marketing is always a refining process. Keep in mind that each show has its own style. If the show has been in business for several years it has built up its own clientele so the customers who return each year expect to see a certain type of craft and usually a particular range in price. It is also true that the craftsmen who exhibit year after year go expecting a certain type of customer. Both the buyers and sellers have gone through a refining process to match wants.

Do not take it as a personal insult if your work does not sell well. Analyze what your competitors are doing and if they are selling well find out why. It may be that they have been there for the last ten years and 90% of their sales are from repeat customers. Maybe their prices are lower than others, or, or, or.

□   GETTING PEOPLE TO STOP

No sale ever takes place unless you get a customer to stop long enough to look at your work. You do that by getting his attention and you get a person's attention by doing something unusual or having an unusual product.

The Display Booth

The booth sets the whole tone for your product. If it looks inviting and unusual, people will at least stop out of curiosity. Businessmen spend millions of dollars in advertising each year to entice people to stop by their place of business. You don't have to do that, people come to you! But you must get them to stop in. You can't do that by giving out free samples or having a 2 for 1 sale (you could, but don't). Your booth and your product will do the selling for you, if you help!

Match the booth to your product. Your booth is your store and what your store looks like will prepare the customer for the quality of your product and the price it will be. Let me give you two extreme examples. K-Mart and Neiman Marcus both sell shirts, yet you enter K-Mart expecting to buy a low price shirt of average quality. Your mind is pre-programmed to pay between $5 and $10 for a shirt at K-Mart, but would not be shocked to see shirts priced from $35 up at Neiman Marcus.

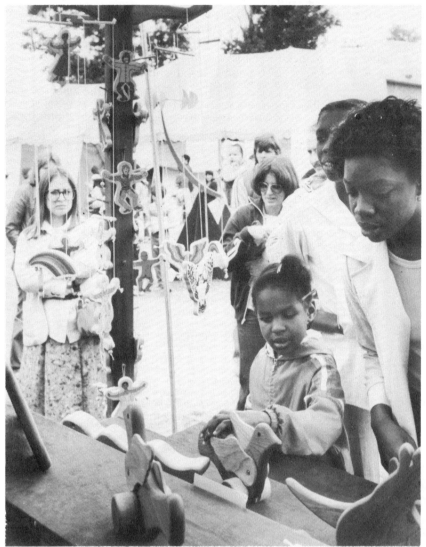

Photographs courtesy of American Craft Enterprises, Inc., P.O. Box 10, New Paltz, NY 12561.

Let's look at two examples of booth designs. The first booth is well designed and encourages customer involvement. Notice that the child is trying out the toy and the adult is interested in how it works! The first step of the display in front is empty in order to provide a play area to see how each toy works. On the tree-like stand to the left are figures; rainbows, owls and other creatures all waiting to travel up the string as soon as someone gives it a gentle pull. Finally, the booth is well-made with the shelves being constructed out of the same wood used to construct the toys.

Photographer, Robert Barrett.

The second display booth also features wood items and is well constructed. However, I feel it would be much more effective if it encouraged more participation. Remember that a customer buys a product because of personal benefit. If the person behind the counter could help the customer visualize how much better it would be cutting vegetables for her favorite soup on that new rosewood cutting board, she would be halfway to a sale.

Demonstrating is an excellent way to attract attention. If people can see how you make or use your product they will stop and ask questions. Plus, if you have all the equipment you need to produce your work at your booth you can do custom work and continue to produce work during slow periods. It helps lower your selling costs.

An unusual, inviting setting is another attention getter. Two craftsmen I saw at one show had their productions of antique furniture on display. Their work was arranged to look like a typical antique shop. When people entered and realized that they were reproductions they bought them like crazy because they were so realistic and excellently priced. The key was the fact that the booth was attractive and helped the customer visualize how these items would look in their own home.

□ ESSENTIALS OF GOOD DISPLAY

Very simply, the quality of the display should match the quality of the work. Just as Neiman Marcus and Saks Fifth Avenue have a particular style so do K-Mart and Woolworth. A production potter can display his low priced items on natural boards and have a very effective display. A craftsman making high-priced, one-of-a-kind jewelry items might display his work in plexiglass boxes mounted on pedestals. People interested in his work have to ask to see it and to have it removed from the case, just as one would expect in a fine jewelry store.

Wooden toys might be displayed in a booth designed to look like a child's room or playground. The bottom line is to create an image.

Combine your effective, image-creating display with ease of transportation and you have a real winner. Some craftsmen have been very clever in combining mobility and ease of set-up and take-down with visual impact. There are several commercial display builders who produce quality stands that you might want to look into.

□ PROMOTING YOUR BUSINESS

Why do some businesses succeed and others fail? There are obviously many reasons, but your chances of failure are 100% if nobody knows you exist, and that's where publicity comes in. Few craftsmen like bookkeeping or all those other "business" things, but they know they have to do them to survive. Publicity is another necessity!

One potter I talked to said she hated writing the little descriptive card that she attaches to her pottery. "It sounds stupid and as if I'm bragging." Lots of craftspeople feel that promoting themselves and their work is "pushy and demeaning"; all they really want to do is make their crafts. The message throughout this book is that you are in the craft business and that means making a living from making crafts and that is never going to happen without a lot of publicity and promotion. If you absolutely hate promoting yourself, hire someone to do it for you, but do it!

Your job is to attract customers. You can call it marketing, promotion, public relations, publicity, creative advertising or showmanship or whatever you want to. It all adds up to the same thing — attracting customers.

Do you know what the Small Business Administration has identified as one of the most common problems of small business? Failure of small business to understand the importance of being attractively different. Even fewer think of the small things they can do to bring the best kind of free publicity to back up their paid advertising.

The first thing you need to do is decide what is unique about you and your product, your positioning theme. This is the feature you will advertise and promote. And then be as creative as you can be.

If you are a potter, you probably make a lot of mugs. Mugs sell for pretty much the same price around the country and are available in all shapes and sizes. Did you ever think about the most important selling point of a mug? How it feels in the hand and, most importantly, how it feels to the fingers. How about advertising your cups as "finger fitted"? In a large urban area you could probably attract enough customers to your studio to make it highly profitable. Customers might come by appointment only and have their mug custom fitted for them. Naturally you would sign them on the bottom and write especially fitted for George White (or whatever). You would also have a card with the shape and size of the cup and handle recorded. You would also have made two cups exactly alike. When the customer came to pick up the cup you would tell him/her that they could choose either one and that you'd keep the other one on hand in case they wanted another or the first one broke.

The next step is to contact newspapers and magazines in your area and tell them about your unique service. The articles may have a heading like: "He Makes the Most Comfortable Cups in the World." The story would go on to describe how you custom fit each cup to the customer, that everyone has different-sized hands, that left-handed people hold their cups differently from right-handed people, etc., etc.

If you are a weaver, you might custom design wall hangings, place mats, pillows and clothing for individuals. Color plays such an important part in our personalities that you could advertise that you color match to the client's needs.

If you are a jeweler, what is unique about your products? Can you custom design? Can you incorporate stones from other jewelry? Do you use a unique or unusual process? What can you think of?

Here are some ways that other businesses have attracted customers:

•A cranberry sauce maker offered a plastic cutter that would cut slices of cranberry jelly into the shape of a turkey. All people had to do was send in a label from the can of cranberry sauce and 10¢. They were swamped with replies — up to 10,000 a week.

•A restaurant changed its name from Tea Room to Restaurant and increased its sales ten times.

•A delicatessen owner called his restaurant the Rolls-Royce of delicatessens and had it printed on his matchbooks, menus, and brochures. He charges more and his customers love it!

•A real estate salesman always double priced his apartments. He'd advertise two identical apartments, but across the hall from each other. One would be 10% higher per month than the other. The salesman listened to the couple's reaction; if they talked about how good a buy the cheaper apartment was, he'd emphasize that this was the last apartment available at that price. If the couple liked the prestige of having the most expensive apartment in the building he would work on what status that would bring them. Moral: Are you selling price or prestige?

•A young entrepreneur started a restaurant with the unique idea of baking bread in clay flower pots. The idea caught on so well that she had to open another restaurant and was recently offered a million dollars for her idea and name by a large restaurant chain.

•A couple, fed up with working for other people, opened a bakery using no preservatives. People throughout the country with special dietary needs order their products.

•We all have read about the resurgence of the chimney sweep, dressed in top hat and tails. If that isn't a promotional device, I don't know what is.

There are many more innovative ideas that people have used. They have all used the same process to make their business unique. Remember what the S.B.A. identified as the most common problem of small business? *Failure of small business to understand the important of being attractively different.* Here's a checklist to help you find your promotional, customer-attracting uniqueness.

1. Personal: What's different or unusual about you?

2. Location: Is there anything unusual about the location of your business? For example, one gallery I sell to has its studio and gallery in an old mill. They advertise this heavily in their promotional literature.

3. Material: Do you use rare or hard-to-get materials? One jeweler uses quahog shells (not rare, but unusual) in his work. His brochure describes how these shells were used by American Indians as an early form of money (wampum), and then describes

how they are fashioned into jewelry.

---

4. Process: Do you use a unique or long-lost process? This is a natural for craftsmen because people are always fascinated by our hand-made processes.

I know you can create your own "attractively different" promotional campaign. You are using your positioning theme to find your hole in the marketplace.

A wooden toy maker in New Jersey has the right idea by picturing himself in his sales brochure. If Santa Claus has a twin brother, this craftsman has to be him. His white full beard and rotund body is suitably attired in overalls. He has excellent potential for developing a positioning theme.

□ PROMOTIONAL OUTLETS

Let's get down to the nitty gritty and identify the biggest obstacle to successful promotion of your crafts business: YOU. That's right, YOU. The truth is that as a craftsman you are a very unique individual and are newsworthy. How often have you read about someone who received a promotion, graduated from the service, got married, opened a new business, etc., etc.? Your activities as a craftsman can be much more newsworthy than these items. Also, did you know that almost all of these news announcements were initiated by the individual or by a close associate, not by the newspaper?

The secret to successful promotion is similar to successful marketing; having the right product, in the right place at the right time. Here's how it works:

The Right Product

Any promotional outlet, radio, TV, newspapers, magazines, newsletters, direct mail, etc., etc., is always looking for unusual news items. Obviously you are unusual because of your craft talents but you must convey that to others. In the publicity field it's called a hook or attention grabber. As I wrote this I looked in the newspaper and found:

1. An article on how homeowners can sell their homes by taking a second mortgage from the buyer was entitled: "A Second Chance for Buyers."

2. An article on how Army bomb experts detonated a suspicious, ticking package and later found it to be a Pac-Mac game was entitled: "Army Takes on Pac-Man, Contest Ends with a Bang."

There were many more but let's see how the same approach works in the crafts area. I mentioned earlier the toy maker in New Jersey. Here are two headlines for a newspaper article or TV story:

New Jersey Man Makes Toys Out of Wood
Meets New Jersey's 365 Day Santa Claus

Which one would turn you on? Here are two to choose from for a weaver who uses natural dyes she produces from local plants, fruits and vegetables:

Weaver Produces Range of Hand-Made Items
This Weaver Makes Her Living Dyeing, Naturally!

Shall we try one more? I use local Georgia clay for much of my work. The stuff is everywhere in Georgia. In fact, most of the soil in Georgia is red because of its high iron and clay content. An announcement about a gallery show might read:

Local Potter to Exhibit
Georgia Clay Elevated to Fine Art Status

You can see the difference an interesting headline makes. It also gives you the direction the rest of the news announcement should take.

Yes, you write the article, because nobody knows more about your business than you do. Your objective is to interest your news outlet in your story. They will decide to use it as is, not use it at all, or adapt it to fit their editorial style. At times they will send a reporter to do a full scale feature on you. But, you need to contact them first, according to their rules. Your story can be essentially the same for any outlet you choose; a headline that is a grabber, followed by details about you and your unique activities. However, the way you approach each outlet varies.

The Right Place

Regardless of what outlet you select you should do all you can to make a personal contact. People in the news business get to know each other so an art editor for the city newspaper knows the person to contact at the TV station regarding your crafts release. The point is to use your contacts, but first you need to have contacts. Here's how to get in touch with the right people in:

The weekly newspapers. These are usually local papers dealing with the news and events in a well defined local area. Look through several issues of the newspaper and list the names of the reporters who wrote articles on arts and crafts events. In most cases the weekly papers are small; only one reporter is assigned to cover a certain range of subjects. Once the reporter has been identified give him or her a call (an advice call) and say, "Ms. Newsworthy? My name is _____

_____. I'm writing a news release on the unique crafts business I have and wanted to get your advice. I've read your articles on other craftspeople and have really enjoyed them. Could I send the news release directly to you? You might be able to point out some things that I should have included. Anyway, I'd really appreciate your reactions."

The daily newspapers. Use the same research process as with the weekly newspapers to identify the art editor or reporter. Sometimes the newspaper will list its staff on the editorial page. Call the art reporter and use the same advice call approach as with the weekly paper. The important thing to keep in mind is that you are making a personal contact and when your photo and story does reach his desk he is going to remember you.

Radio. Many radio stations do public service announcements free. Radio managers will promote a craft fair or show but will seldom agree to announce your gallery opening or your participation at a craft fair.

However, there are some promotional techniques that you can take advantage of through radio. Most radio stations publish a program calendar listing their monthly schedule of programs. Give the station a call and ask for a copy. Look it over carefully to see if there are any programs that you might fit in. Programs like "News Around the State," "The Arts Report", "People in the News", etc., offer ideal opportunities for you to tell people about your crafts business. Remember to have a hook or original slant to your story.

Television. Living in an area, you probably know who deals with the arts on television. This person is the one you should contact for an advice call. Tell him who you are and what you want and ask for his advice. He should have at least two or three people that he knows who would be interested in your story. A personal phone call is the best approach but if you are unable to get through send a letter. Here are some other approaches to use for the television promotional outlet:

1. Contact the program director, tell him what you do and ask him if he thinks the viewers would be interested in your craft. He will probably ask you to send in a proposal for a program or segment so have your information ready.
2. Look through the program directory and choose the programs that deal with news about people.
3. Watch the programs you have selected and see how they deal with various topics. When you contact the director of the program tailor your approach to match the format of the program. You'll have a much better chance of getting on the air.
4. Watch for special seasonal program announcements. A story on your lace snowflakes may not be newsworthy in July but certainly would be in December.
5. Watch for special news events that you can tie into. If there is a showing of fabrics at the local museum maybe you can use your experience as a weaver to show how the fabrics were

made. Shortly after the last eruption of Mount St. Helens a potter gained publicity by letting everyone know that he was using volcanic ash in his glazes. Television stations like to have local tie-ins with national stories. Use your imagination to promote your business.

Television, radio, newspapers and magazines all use fillers. News about your business may be used as a filler for a slow news day. Don't be surprised if they do a story about you and don't use it for a month or more. It will still be good publicity when they do use it.

Magazines. Again, research helps here. I use a standard news release to send to the magazines I feel would be interested in what I do but, and here's what really makes the big difference, I send a personalized cover letter addressed to a specific person at the magazine. Sometimes it's the editor-in-chief, sometimes it's the editor of a particular section of the magazine. Use your discretion on this one but be sure that you address a particular individual.

Most magazines will send you a complimentary copy of the issue they published your news release in. That's one of the best deals in town; free publicity and a free magazine. By all means write back and thank the editor who published your news. I wait about a month so I can inform the editor about how much response I got from the news release. They like to know what their readers respond to and if it is a good response chances are that they will print some more of your news releases, if they are truly newsworthy.

Magazines have tremendous power because they have large circulations and they generate response over a long period of time because people tend to keep magazines and look at them again and again. Remember, however, that it takes three to four months for your article to be published. If you want publicity for something that you'll be doing for the Christmas season you had better send your information in August.

☐ OTHER PROMOTIONAL AIDS

The more your name is exposed the better your business will be. Here are some simple things that you can do that will help.

Business Cards

Have them with you at all times and pass them out freely. They are very inexpensive and are extremely effective advertising devices.

Do not ask any of your wholesale outlets (galleries, shops, department stores, etc., etc.) to pass out your cards. They want people to return to their store to buy your work. Why should they pass out your card with your name and address on it so the customer can buy directly from you?

Another approach is much better for wholesale outlets.

The Brochure

A brochure tells about you and your work. They come in all shapes and sizes. Take your time to design an impressive one and have a couple thousand (at least) printed up! Now, here's the trick. At the end of the brochure leave a little room. When you establish a wholesale account, go to a local printer and have a rubber stamp made with the name and address of the wholesale outlet on it. Then, with each order you ship to that outlet include some brochures stamped on the bottom. Your stamp should read something like this:

This Artist's Work Featured At

The Butterfly Gallery
2232 Lanier St.
McGregor, GA 30083

(404) 681-5532

Now you have the best of both worlds. You are getting excellent publicity and so is the gallery. Galleries and other outlets like this idea so much they often imprint the brochures of all the artists they feature. That's fine! The idea is not original with me. It's just an idea that works so why not use it?

□   CLOSING THE SALE

It doesn't make any difference if you like to call it exchange function or getting the money, it is still the most important part of the whole marketing process because without some sort of exchange of money no sale ever takes place. So, here are some things to consider in retail selling.

Be prepared to accept credit cards! Prominently display the cards that you do accept in the sales area. Some customers will assume that you don't accept credit cards unless the card is displayed and many will not buy unless they can charge the sale on their card.

Checks are also common and you should be prepared to accept them with proper identification.

In some of the larger metropolitan areas you can subscribe to a service that allows you to check the validity of credit cards and checks simply by running the card or driver's license through a machine or calling a credit verification number. If your studio is in such an area it might be a good idea to subscribe to such a service.

You have to take your chances when doing the craft fair or mall show. It's often difficult to check a person's credit when you are in the middle of a field surrounded by thousands of people. However, if the purchase is a substantial one you can protect yourself by asking the customer to return for his/her purchase in an hour or so, allowing you time to get to a phone and call in for a credit check.

□ MATCHING YOUR IMAGE TO THE MARKET

Retail marketing as we have defined it here consists of many different marketing channels and the image you portray will be different in each channel. It probably will be similar in the craft fair and mall show markets because in both you will portray yourself as a serious independent craftsman. Obviously you will have made the items on display in your booth but you will not be making any while you are selling so you can dress casually but neatly.

Selling from the studio necessitates that you work there as well. Therefore, people entering the shop will expect to see you in work clothes. Just as you would not expect to visit a dentist's office and see him dressed in blue jeans, you would not expect to visit a crafts studio expecting to see the owner dressed in a suit or business dress. Play the role.

□ PREPARING YOUR RESUME

A resume is simply a list of all your accomplishments, so the first thing you need to do is sit down and list everything that you have done in the craft business. Don't leave anything out! If you helped organize craft fairs for a craft association list that. If you have given talks or demonstrations list those. List the shows that you have exhibited in, the awards you have had and any education that relates to your profession. Think of your resume as a job application; you are applying for a job selling your work.

After you have listed all your accomplishments it's time to arrange them for maximum impact in a particular market channel. Preparing an effective resume is simple if you just tell your audience what they want to hear. Let's say that you have been in the craft business for 20 years and have experience in every marketing channel. When you apply to a craft fair you design a resume that lists the fairs that you have exhibited at first, and then include any other supportive information that you want to include. Why? Because this is a resume designed to be looked at by craft fair promoters and they are looking for people who have experience in selling at craft shows.

If you were selling primarily from your studio you must prepare your resume to describe your studio, how you came to open it, why you have chosen this way of life and then list some of your accomplishments. Why? Because the typical customer who stops by your studio wants to know more about you as a person than as an artist. Many of the pieces purchased at your studio will be used as gifts so if the purchaser can include a little brochure (resume) about you the person receiving the gift will be impressed with the thoughtfulness of the gift giver.

The next two pages illustrate resumes for both the craft fair and studio sales. Both resumes are those of the same craftsman but have been tailored to fit a particular market channel.

RESUME

Alan Potter

Personal Data:

Alan W. Potter

6184 Cedar Crest Drive

Wareham, Massachusetts 02571

617-251-8865

Exhibition Record:

The Fair at Rhinebeck

The Fair at Baltimore

Georgia Mountain Jubilee

Prater's Mill Country Fair

Power's Crossing Craft Fair

New England Craft Fair

Spring Arts and Crafts Festival

American Designer Craftsman

Plus 10-15 regional and local shows each year

Other Achievements:

Work exhibited in over 40 galleries and private

collections through the United States.

Educational Background:

Bachelor of Fine Arts Degree, Massachusetts College

of Fine Arts, 1975

Numerous workshops, demonstrations and seminars

attended throughout the country.

CROOKED CREEK STUDIO

Crooked Creek Studio is owned and operated by Alan
Potter. The studio is located in an old mill and features
the work of Alan Potter and other fine craftsmen.

Alan Potter has been a craftsman for over 10 years.
He graduated with a degree in painting but soon discovered
that making pottery offered the creative challenge that he
wanted. Eight years ago Alan bought the old mill that is
now the Crooked Creek Studio and has been making his living
as a full time potter ever since. His work is highly regarded
because of its unusual design and glaze treatment. Each piece
is individually designed and signed and is crafted entirely
in the Crooked Creek Studio.

Alan welcomes visitors to his studio during business
hours and takes pleasure in demonstrating his skills and
talking about his work.

Alan's work has been exhibited in over 40 galleries and
private collections. In addition to selling at his studio
Alan sells his work at selected craft shows each year,
including The Fair at Baltimore and The Fair at Dallas.

Studio Hours:

    Monday through Friday
    (closed Wednesday) 10:00-5:00

    Saturday 9:00-6:00

    Sunday 1:00-5:00

Location:

    Crooked Creek Studio is located on Rt. 3 in Wareham,
    Massachusetts. The address is:

        6184 Cedar Crest Drive

        Wareham, Massachusetts 02571

        617-251-8865

Chapter 8

Market Profile: The Craft Fair/Mall Show

☐ APPLYING TO A SHOW

1. Read the application. This sounds obvious, but lots of people don't. It is a fairly safe bet that the sponsors of the show developed the application form because they wanted to have certain information to help them make their decisions. If you don't fill it out properly, they have every right to deny you admission; and they will! Fill it out neatly and legibly. Your application form, along with anything else you send, gives the judges an impression, good or bad, of you. Make it good.
2. Include a business card. Even if they don't ask for it, send one. It confirms a professional interest in crafts.
3. Include color slides if requested. Clear plastic slide holders are available at photo and stationery stores. Send your slides in a holder; it makes them easier to view and protects them in shipping and handling. Write a description of the piece on each slide, including size and material. Also, include your name.

4. Include a self-addressed stamped envelope if requested. Many shows require this so they can notify you of acceptance or

rejection. They have the right to keep your slides if you fail to include a SASE.

5. Send in your application fee. It doesn't matter if it's a judging fee or a booth fee, your application will not be processed unless you include your fee. If your application is rejected, the booth fee will be refunded.

6. Include a resume. This resume should list your previous participation in craft shows. I'd even list the fairs in order of prestige. For example:

EXHIBITION EXPERIENCE:

The Fair at Rhinebeck, 1984	Sales...................$3,725
The Baltimore Winter Market, 1983	Sales...................$4,784
The Georgia Mountain Show, 1976	Sales...................$2,000
Etc. Etc.	

Use discretion on the sales figures. If they are impressive, use them. If they are low leave them off. Use only what will work to your benefit.

7. Send everything in a neat package. Initial impressions are important. A neat package says, "here is a craftsman who cares about himself and his work." It gives a much more favorable impression than a crumpled up old stained envelope with the address scribbled in pencil. The envelope need not be typed, but it should be neatly addressed and should include your return address.

□   TYPICAL APPLICATION FORMS

Illustrated below are forms typical of those you will be sent.

Membership Application

American Craft Enterprises, Inc. presents major crafts shows in Springfield, Mass., San Francisco, Calif., Dallas Tex., Baltimore, Md., and others. These shows are sponsored by the American Crafts Council, the parent organization of American Craft Enterprises, Inc. The shows are open only to members of the American Crafts Council. Membership in the American Crafts Council not only entitles you to apply for ACE shows, but you also receive their excellent magazine and other benefits.

Shows restricted to members only are not unusual. Many state and regional craft organizations have the same requirement for the shows they sponsor. Any application you receive will specify membership requirements if any. It is generally agreed that membership-only shows tend to be of a better quality than others. So, it may be worthwhile to join an active organization in your area.

AMERICAN CRAFT COUNCIL
401 PARK AVENUE SOUTH
NEW YORK, NY 10016
(212) 696-0710

AMERICAN CRAFT MAGAZINE
401 PARK AVENUE SOUTH
NEW YORK, NY 10016
(212) 696-0710

AMERICAN CRAFT MUSEUM
44 WEST 53 STREET
NEW YORK, NY 10019
(212) 397-0630

AMERICAN CRAFT ENTERPRISES, INC.
PO BOX 10
NEW PALTZ, NEW YORK 12561
(914) 255-0039

The American Craft Council is a national, nonprofit membership organization founded in 1943 to promote interest in contemporary crafts. ACC maintains the American Craft Museum in New York City, publishes the magazine AMERICAN CRAFT and sponsors a library and nationwide audiovisual service. Through the subsidiary, American Craft Enterprises, Inc., ACC presents craft markets in various parts of the country. Membership in the American Craft Council is open to all.

LEVELS OF MEMBERSHIP   BENEFITS OF MEMBERSHIP IN THE AMERICAN CRAFT COUNCIL

Member   Domestic   ˙Subscription to AMERICAN CRAFT magazine
            $29.50 - 1 yr   ˙Free admission American Craft Museum I
            $55   - 2 yr   (44 West 53rd Street) and American Craft
            $22   - student   Museum II (International Paper Plaza, West
            (with copy of   45th Street, New York City)
            i.d. card)   ˙Free use of the American Craft Council Library-
            Foreign   (44 West 53rd Street)
            $33   -1 yr   ˙Discounts on ACC publications, exhibition
            $61   -2 yr   catalogs and slides
            $27   -student   ˙Eligibility to apply for group insurance
            (with copy of   ˙Free admission to craft markets sponsored by
            i.d. card)   American Craft Enterprises, Inc.
                                     ˙An ACC membership card
                                     ˙A vote in the ACC annual election

Contributor $ 50   Additional Benefits to Contributors
                                     ˙Complimentary copy of new American Craft
                                     Museum exhibition catalogs on request

Sponsor $100   Additional Benefits to Sponsors, Friends,
Friend $250   Patrons and Benefactors
Patron $500
Benefactor $1,000
             or more   ˙Invitations to private exhibition previews
                                     ˙Invitations to other special events
                                     sponsored by the American Craft Council
                                     ˙Complimentary copy of new American Craft
                                     Museum exhibition catalogs

---

Tear Off to Mail
MEMBERSHIP ENROLLMENT FORM

NAME_____   Please make checks payable to the
ADDRESS_____   American Craft Council in U.S. funds.
CITY_____   Allow 8-10 weeks to receive your
STATE_____ZIP_____   first copy of AMERICAN CRAFT.
SIGNATURE_____$____   American Craft Council
                                              Membership Dept.
                                              PO Box 1308-CL
                                              Fort Lee, NJ 07024

Contributions are deductible within legal limits for tax purposes   8RB2

<u>RULES AND REGULATIONS</u>

<u>OF AMERICAN CRAFT ENTERPRISES MARKETING EVENTS</u>

1. If an exhibitor cancels, after making a definite reservation, the space fee--less $25--will be refunded, provided A.C.E. can resell the booth space to a 'waiting list' craftsperson. However, if an exhibitor cancels within 14 days prior to the opening day of the event, the space fee--less $50--will be refunded, provided A.C.E. can resell the booth space to a 'waiting list' craftsperson.

2. All exhibitors should be professional in their field, be capable of filling orders, and be responsible for commitments made at the event. Failure to fulfill commitments may exclude exhibitors from future A.C.E. events.

3. Students engaged full-time in their educational activity should not exhibit in an American Craft Enterprises event.

4. Sales representatives or agents who sell craft work but are not directly involved in the production of that work may not participate in the event.

5. All work exhibited in the event must be made by hand (or with the use of appropriate tools) by the craftsperson accompanying it to the event.

6. All exhibitors must be in attendance during the event, and all booths must remain intact until the conclusion of the event.

7. All exhibitors must contain their display, their work, and their storage boxes within the dimensions of the space they rent. (Additional storage space at some events may be provided by A.C.E.)

8. Exhibitors are responsible for the back and/or outside of their booths to the extent that these areas be visually presentatble to the neighboring exhibitor(s).

9. Exhibitors' booths must be of sound construction and must in no way obstruct or endanger the neighboring booth areas.

10. Any handmade object which is contained in an exhibitor's booth and which is for sale, or has sales literature attached to it, must be made solely by the exhibiting crafts-person.

11. Each exhibitor may exhibit in his or her booth only the <u>type of work</u> which appeared in the slides submitted to the Selection Committee by that exhibitor. A.C.E. re-serves the right to require that work not of that type be removed from the booth or that the entire booth be removed from the event.

12. All work exhibited in the event must be made in America. Objects assembled from a commercially sold kit may not be exhibited. Kits designed to produce an object may not be exhibited. Objects that are created by adherence to commercially avail-able plans may not be exhibited. Objects which fall into categories described as ineligible in our Application Information Sheet may not be exhibited.

13. American Craft Enterprises is not responsible for loss, theft or damage to an exhib-itor's work during the event. Each exhibitor exhibits at his or her own risk.

In order to maintain the standards and quality of the event, we reserve the right to require any exhibitor violating the above rules and regulations to conform to these standards, or the right to prohibit the craftsperson from exhibiting.

Rules and Regulations

Any show specifies what you can and cannot do. The rules are for your protection and for the protection of the show committee. Read them carefully before you sign, but you will not find anything that will disturb you. If you do, ask about it and if it still disturbs you, don't exhibit.

SLIDE CARD

See directions on reverse side.

Top

| CODE # | CODE # |

Bottom

| CODE # | CODE # | CODE # |

Booth Display

CODE # *1 X 95*   VIEWING #

DIRECTIONS

1. Send four (4) slides of your work, all being a representation of the work you will be showing.

2. Send one (1) slide of your booth display.

3. Place the above code number on the top of each of the five (5) slides submitted.

4. Return both your application and this slide card in the return envelope provided. Be sure to complete the front of the envelope by placing your name and address, code number and media **all** in the spaces provided.

5. All applications must be post marked no later than November 1, 1984.

6. Applicants will be notified of their status no later than December 15, 1984.

NAME _____

ADDRESS _____

CITY _____

STATE _____ ZIP _____

Jury Application

All quality shows are juried. You will be asked to submit slides (almost always) or photos of your work. The panel of judges review your work to decide whether you will be accepted. Very often a non-refundable jury fee is required, ranging from $5 to $25. This fee should be sent with your slides and application.

 **AMERICAN CRAFT ENTERPRISES, INC.**
P.O. Box 10, New Paltz, New York 12561 / (914) 255-0039

EXHIBITOR CONTRACT and DIRECTORY LISTING FORM

Please complete the following carefully, print clearly or type. Return top two copies with your space payment, and ACC membership application or proof of ACC membership, no later than date specified. Keep third copy for your records.

Update Any Incorrect Information Specified Below

The following is a list of categories used in our Official Show Directory. Please indicate in which categories you wish to be listed.

CERAMICS
☐ Architectural
☐ Non-Utilitarian/Sculptural
☐ Functional
☐ Earthenware
☐ Porcelain
☐ Raku
☐ Salt-Glazed
☐ Stoneware
☐ Pitfired

FIBER
☐ Applique/Patchwork
☐ Banners
☐ Batik
☐ Canvas
☐ Clothing
☐ Crochet
☐ Dolls/Puppets
☐ Felting
☐ Hats/Bags/Access.
☐ Knitted

☐ Macrame
☐ Painted/Silk Screened
☐ Quilts
☐ Rugs
☐ Soft Sculpture
☐ Trapunto
☐ Wall Hangings
☐ Weaving

GLASS
☐ Blown
☐ Etched
☐ Lampwork
☐ Stained
☐ Leaded

JEWELRY
☐ Precious Metal
☐ Other Metal
☐ Enamel/Cloisonne
☐ Scrimshaw/Ivory
☐ Non-Metal

LEATHER
☐ Accessories
☐ Clothing
☐ Sheepskin
☐ Toys

METAL
☐ Bells
☐ Flatware
☐ Forged Iron/Blacksmithing
☐ Holloware
☐ Knives
☐ Pewter
☐ Sculptural
☐ Tinsmithing

WOOD
☐ Accessories
☐ Furniture
☐ Sculptural
☐ Toys

ADDITIONAL
☐ Adult Toys
☐ Basketry
☐ Bookbinding
☐ Brooms
☐ Candles
☐ Clocks
☐ Electronic Art
☐ Feathers
☐ Hammocks/Hanging Chairs
☐ Kaleidoscopes
☐ Luggage
☐ Marionettes
☐ Musical Instruments
☐ Paper-Handmade/Handscreened
☐ Paper Reliefs
☐ Pipes

BOOTH SIGN should read (limit 20 spaces):

☐ ☐ ☐ ☐ ☐ ☐ ☐ ☐ ☐ ☐ ☐ ☐ ☐ ☐ ☐ ☐ ☐ ☐ ☐ ☐

☐ I have not exhibited in A.C.E. events previously and would like to receive information for new exhibitors.

I have read the rules and regulations of American Craft Enterprises, Inc. on the back of this contract and agree to abide by them as an exhibitor.

_____   _____   _____
Signature of Exhibitor   Date   Signature of Director

Show Contract

You have been accepted! Now you must sign the contract acknowledging that you understand and agree to abide by the rules and regulations of the show committee. Send your booth fee with the signed contract to insure that you have a space reserved for you. It is possible to pull out later if there is an emergency and get part, if not all, of your booth fee refunded.

CRAFT_____ WHOLESALE SALES & ORDERS: $_____

RETAIL SALES AND RETAIL ORDERS TAKEN AT MARKET: $_____.

We are attempting to gather some information on the business aspect of crafts. We hope you will help by spending a few moments of your time to complete this questionnaire.

1. Please check which craft(s) you offered for sale at the Market:

___baskets   ___wall hangings   ___jewelry-precious metal
___ceramics, non-utilitarian   ___weaving, non-clothing ___jewelry-other materials
___ceramics, functional   ___blown glass   ___sculptural metals
___fiber clothing   ___stained glass   ___musical instruments
___crochet   ___leather   ___wood accessories
___dolls, puppets   ___enamels   ___furniture
___quilts, patch, applique   ___holloware   ___sculptural wood
___soft sculpture   ___forged iron   ___wood toys
        other_____

2. Have you exhibited in this fair before?   ____YES ____NO
    How many times?   ____

3. Have you exhibited in other A.C.E. events before? ____YES ____NO
    How many in the past year?   ____
    How many in total?   ____

4. What other fairs do you exhibit in?

    _____   _____

    _____   _____

    _____   _____

5. How many fairs do you do in one year?   ____

6. How long have you been selling your work?   ____ years

7. What percentage of your total income is earned
    from the sale of crafts?   ____ %

(Over, please)

Other Forms

Each show has its unique forms so you may see a strange one here or there, but usually they are very simple. Some shows may require you to fill out a state and local sales tax form, or may request your business license number (if you have one).

Post-market questionnaire

8. What is the retail price range of the crafts you offered for sale at the Market?

    Lowest retail price: $_____   Highest retail price: $_____

9. What was the <u>average</u> price of the works you sold at the Market?

    $ _____

10. Do you consign work to shops?   ____YES   ____NO

11. Please estimate the retail dollar volume of sales of consigned work, if you consign.

    $ _____

12. What other methods do you use for selling your work?

    ___direct calls on shops   ___showrooms

    ___direct mail orders   ___catalog distributions

    ___sales representatives   ___other fairs

                                      _____other

13. What changes have you noticed in the past year with regard to your customers' buying habits?

Thank you for your assistance; we are grateful for your help. Please use the rest of the space here to make your suggestions and/or comments with regard to this year's craft market.

                              AMERICAN CRAFT ENTERPRISES, INC.

□   MARKET STRATEGIES

One of the things you quickly learn in the craft business is that each market channel is different and the approach to selling in each channel has to be tailored to that particular channel. The simple fact is that people buy for different reasons in different market channels and if you are not appealing to their wants in that particular channel your sales will not be impressive.

As you gain experience in each market channel you will develop specific marketing plans for each outlet within a particular market channel. Instead of having a selling plan for shows in general, you will have a selling plan for each specific show because you will know from experience what works best for each particular show. Obviously this is the ideal situation, but it will take some time and experience to develop. Let's begin by looking at the show as a marketing channel.

It is appropriate to be reminded here that people buy crafts because they satisfy *their* wants and needs, not yours. Many craftsmen, particularly in the beginning, believe that because they put so much time, effort and love into their creations, everyone who sees them will immediately buy. It doesn't take long to realize that a craft product, like any other product, must compete in the marketplace and will only sell if it meets a customer's want or need.

Most people go to most fairs because they are fun! They go to look at crafts, but also to eat, watch the contests and see people. Most people do not have a specific item in mind when they tour the craft displays, they are window shopping. Your job is to get them to stop at your booth and at least look at what you have. Any selling that occurs takes place after you have their attention.

You have a little different audience at a mall show. Usually people are there primarily to shop at the regular stores in the mall. Your presence is only a happy surprise. What craft buying they do they usually do on impulse. Regardless of market channel the bottom line still remains the same — getting customers to stop, look, feel and buy your crafts.

□   COMPETITION

Whatever market channel you choose, you'll be in competition with other craftsmen. People are careful shoppers and always compare values so if you are offering more value for the money than fellow craftsmen, you should be in good shape in the marketplace.

Assume the role of the consumer and visit all the craftsmen exhibiting with you at the show. Your objective is to evaluate the competition so you can see where you fit and can take steps to improve your market position.

Earlier, you wrote a positioning statement for your craft. Do a similar report for each one of your competitors. The more you know about them, the more effectively you will be able to compete with them. Here's a form you might use.

COMPETITORS POSITIONING REPORT

Name of Business _____

Initial Impression _____

_____

Impressions After Survey_____

_____

Positioning Theme _____

_____

_____

Show Compatibility _____

_____

_____

Effective Marketing Strategies _____

_____

_____

Ineffective Marketing Strategies _____

_____

_____

Price/Quality Assessment _____

_____

Do an analysis for each craftsman producing pieces similar to yours. Simply going through the process will help you become more aware of what is available to customers in your craft area and will suggest strategies that might be effective at this particular show.

Let's look at the Competitors Positioning Report and see how a typical one might be filled out.

Business name. This is pretty straightforward. Include address and determine if the name reflects the type of craft.

Positioning theme. Not every booth you visit will have one and some will never have thought about it. Regardless, try to determine what's unique about the work, the anticipated audience, and whether the booth is designed to attract that audience.

Show compatibility. Not every market is suitable for every craft and vice-versa. Is this craftsman where he should be? Perhaps he has the right market but this show is wrong.

Effective marketing strategies. What is being done to increase business? Are there demonstrations, business cards, easy access to the booth, etc.?

Ineffective marketing strategies. Does the craftsman look bored, are the items hard to get to or look at, is the entrance inviting, etc., etc.?

Price/quality evaluation. How does the craftsman's work compare to yours and others at the show? If it's better-crafted at a lower price, you have some real competition; if yours is better-crafted at a similar price, you can use that in your sales dialogue.

Competition, generally, is good for you because it sharpens your craft and marketing skills. Plus, the fact that many craftsmen gathered together in one place is responsible for the large show attendance. Very few people would come to a show if they knew it was going to be a single craftsman in a booth in the middle of a field or mall.

□   LOCATING MARKET OPPORTUNITIES

All craft shows require applications in advance. It is not uncommon, particularly in the case of quality shows, to submit applications two months before the actual show date. This allows time for judging, organization and publicity.

Obviously, it takes advance planning to meet application deadlines and have the required inventory ready when the show does arrive. Many craftsmen use a master calendar to keep track of upcoming events and deadlines. It's a simple matter to get a large calendar at an office supply store, write in the shows you want to attend as well as the deadline for application and deadline for receipt of entry fee. It helps if you color code the items so that all the dates in red refer to one show, all the dates in blue another, etc., etc.

Here's a technique that works to keep you informed of future shows. Remember that when you see a show or an announcement for a show it is often too late to apply, so have a batch of postcards printed:

Dear Sirs:

I am interested in exhibiting at your show next year. Would you please put me on your mailing list and send me an application form? Thank you for your consideration.

Sincerely,
Your Name and
Address

Pop them in the mail when you see an announcement for a crafts show you might be interested in. This works well because the applications always come in plenty of time for you to fit them into your schedule.

Here are some other approaches:

Weekly Newspapers

The local weeklies always carry announcements of small craft shows. Usually these are open shows. As mentioned earlier, small, open shows are not lucrative, but they can be a good place to start or test new products.

Daily Newspapers

They carry announcements, but often too late for the craftsperson to apply. I live in Atlanta, which has one large show each year called the Piedmont Arts Festival. It is held in a large park in the middle of the city and attracts thousands of people. The local paper starts publicizing it heavily two or three weeks before it begins and on opening day, publishes a map and complete calendar of events. This is all very helpful, but is of no use to the craftsman who wants to exhibit, as their applications had to be in three months earlier. Here's where the postcard technique comes in handy. The newspaper will tell you who is in charge of the show. Send them a postcard *now* so you get on the list next year. In the meantime, check out the current show and see if you really want to be a part of it.

Regional Magazines

These are very helpful, but usually announce the event a month or a few weeks ahead of time . . . . too late to apply for admission. Get out the postcards and send them to interesting looking shows.

Arts Organizations

State arts organizations and state and regional craft associations are very helpful in informing you about crafts shows. Contact them and tell them what you want. Better yet, join an active craft association in your area.

Craft Magazines

Craft magazines in your craft type will always feature news of upcoming craft shows and in plenty of time to apply. *Ceramics Monthly* for potters, and *Fine Woodworking* for woodworkers are just two examples. There is a complete list in the back of this book.

Crafts Marketing Magazines

These magazines are dedicated to helping the serious craftsperson sell his or her work. The best one, in my opinion, is *The Crafts Report*; 700 Orange Street; P.O. Box 1992; Wilmington, Delaware 19899. It lists crafts shows throughout the country and includes the contact person's name and address as well as the attendance figures from last year's show. *Sunshine Artists* does a similar job of listing crafts shows and also includes evaluations of shows; what the good and the bad features are and how the sales were! Contact them at: *Sunshine Artists U.S.A.*; 501-503 W. Virginia Ave.; Winter Park, Florida 32789.

One other that I should mention is *The Quality Crafts Market*. It has excellent articles and listings. The address is: 521 Fifth Avenue, Suite 1700, New York, New York 10017.

There are lots of shows and lots of craftsmen applying for spaces. Your chances of being accepted increase greatly if you apply in a professional way, whether you are applying to a craft show around the corner sponsored by the Daughters of the American Revolution or one of the major national shows.

□   PLANNING FUTURE SALES

Regardless of what happens at a show, you must keep accurate records of what you sold and at what price! An additional few minutes should be spent reflecting on what visitors to your booth were looking for but didn't find, looked at and rejected; what competitors sold and didn't sell. In short, look for all the evidence you can gather about what will sell at that show.

I recommend that you write it all down. I use a form called a Craft Show Marketing Report. This insures that I have the information I need about each individual craft fair. This information is particularly helpful because each craft show is different and requires a different marketing strategy. An example of the Craft Show Marketing Report is shown below.

The name and date of the show is listed at the top of the page, providing a convenient reference to prepare for next year. If the sales sheet indicates that you sold 100 honey pots and only 1 porcelain box at last year's Blue Daisy Festival, then you'll know you should have a good selection of honey pots for this year's fair and just a few porcelain boxes.

The Craft Show Marketing Report is designed as a helpful reminder of the characteristics of a particular show. This, in combination with your sales sheet, will help you prepare for next year's show.

CRAFTS SHOW MARKETING REPORT

Name of Show ___Blue Daisy Festival_____

Date___October 15, 1972_____   Attendance___Fair, best on Sunday___

Weather ___Sunny, 68°-72°_____   Booth Location ___Next to food area___

Positive Reactions

Show was well organized. Booth space was prepared and ready to go. Electricity and waste basket provided. Show seemed well publicized and there was ample parking for exhibitors. Show personnel were courteous and helpful.

Negative Reactions

Poor booth location. Long lines waiting to buy food obstructed booth. Other show activities (band concerts, horse pulling, etc.) were too far away from crafts area — taking away customers. Parking poor for customers — had to walk too far to get to activity areas.

General Comments

Second year of show's existence. First time for me. Show has good potential and will likely grow as more people learn of it. Could be more careful in judging exhibitors — some of the work was commercial and poorly done.

Try it again next year. Items in $10-20 range sell best.

☐ THINGS TO DO IN PREPARATION FOR NEXT YEAR

Products to Add

Small items seem to do best. Increase range of cups, mugs, wall plaques and mirrors.

Presentation Ideas

One exhibitor has music and dressed in the costume of a colonial candlemaker. Sales were excellent!

Hand-out Material

There was a wide range available. The most effective pieces included illustrations of the work and ordering information. I talked to one weaver who said 30% of her business came from people who did not buy at the fair but ordered later.

Booth Design

Many excellent ideas! Took photographs of many of them with the owner's permission. Many of them were ingenious in their portability.

Items Requested by Customers

Trivets, salt and pepper shakers, wine coolers and garlic jars.

What the Competition Sold

Ten other potters at the show. Traditional 'earthy' pots did well. Porcelain also sold well. Bright glazes did less well.

□   EVALUATING MARKET CHANNEL SUITABILITY

In my opening remarks at all my crafts marketing workshops, I always make the point that there is a market for everyone's craft. The task is to find the *right* market. Every professional craftsperson I know has had some experience with shows. Some continue to attend shows while some don't because they have found other marketing channels that work better for them. The old marketing adage should always be kept in mind, "If it works do more of it; if it doesn't, try something else."

After you have tried a few shows and analyzed the profitability of this market channel, you have a sound marketing basis to decide if the show circuit is for you. Most craftspeople continue to participate in shows that have proven profitable for them.

If you decide to do the show circuit, it's extremely important to select the right fairs, but it's equally important to have the right kind of crafts. That's why a targeted marketing plan that is constantly reviewed is so vital to your continued success.

As a craftsperson you are trying to find that ideal situation in which you produce objects which you thoroughly enjoy making and which people will buy.

□   LEAVING THE CRAFT SHOW CIRCUIT

If you are not making money at shows, but you are convinced you are making the right kind of object and your crafts are of good quality, then the best thing is to look for other sales channels. You have no obligation to the organizers to participate in future years, though I suggest it is good professional practice to let them know of your decision. If you receive an application (they are usually sent automatically to previous exhibitors), simply return it noted: WILL NOT EXHIBIT THIS YEAR.

When you leave the craft show business, you will at least have developed contacts and sales in other marketing areas.

□   LEGAL OBLIGATIONS

It is not necessary to point out that once you sign a contract to participate in a show you are assuming a legal obligation. You must honor your part of the contract or suffer the penalty. For example, if you simply don't show up, you have no right to expect a refund or any consideration should you decide to enter next year.

Don't kid yourself! Show promoters remember from year to year. Empty booths look bad.

Earlier we reviewed some contracts. There is nothing complex about them. Simply read them carefully, understand what they say and sign if you agree with the terms.

☐ CRAFT SHOW MARKETING REVIEW

1. Juried craft shows offer the best profit potential.
2. Nobody does well at every show, so select the ones that work best for you.
3. Every show is unique, so plan your marketing strategy for each.
4. Apply early to increase your chances of being accepted.
5. Always be professional in your presentation/application regardless of the reputation of the show.
6. Promote yourself and your crafts at the show.
7. Customers buy what they want, not what you want. Look, listen and record what they buy to assist you in making your marketing plans for the future.
8. Your booth should enhance your product, not detract from it.
9. Demonstrations always increase sales.
10. Have business cards, brochures, etc. available to hand out to people who might buy at a later date.
11. Keep records of what sells, at what price, as well as what doesn't sell.
12. Always try a few new shows each year to refine the list of shows in which you want to participate.
13. Always keep recent slides of your work and your display on hand to facilitate applying to new crafts shows.
14. Use every show as an educational experience; learn from your fellow craftsmen.

Chapter 9

Market Profile: Selling From the Studio

Selling from your own studio can be the most financially rewarding marketing strategy, if you get all the pieces together. But it is not all roses, and customers coming to your studio at all hours can be a real drain on your creative energies and production time. Like any marketing channel it requires a real commitment on your part to make it work. Here are some of the factors that you must consider.

□ CREATING AN IMAGE

People come to a craftsman's studio not only to buy crafts but looking for an experience. The more of an experience you can provide the better the sales will be. I'm not suggesting that you stage a happening but be aware of the customer and his feelings and try to make his visit memorable.

John and Glenn LaRowe at Mark of the Potter in the Georgia mountains have created an image that keeps the people coming back for more, year after year. John has a degree in architecture. He used his skills to convert an old mill into a pottery studio, but retained the original architecture. When a customer walks in he is greeted by an impressive array of beams, pulleys and belts, all used in the old mill. As he walks on the wide board floors he is surrounded by pottery neatly displayed on crates and shelves. The LaRowe's have their studio in the rear of the mill so that they can keep track of people in the sales area while they work. If people stay for a while they are invited to step out on the back porch to feed the trout in the stream below.

I first met John and his wife in 1976. My two girls, then 8 and 10, and now both teenagers, still talk about feeding the trout "at that pottery place in the mountains."

Take a few minutes to think about your image. The American spirit of independence is still very much alive and people admire folks doing their own thing. You can use this in your advertising to promote the fact that you have escaped the rat race and are leading the idyllic life as a craftsman. It may not be true that your life is idyllic but conveying a positive image can only help your sales.

□   KEEPING YOUR CUSTOMERS

I will tell you numerous times that keeping a customer is vital to your financial success. Why? Because regardless of the market channels you select, getting the customer to buy the first time is the most difficult marketing job you do and also the most expensive. Whatever you can do to keep a customer satisfied and buying is well worth the effort.

You must get the name and address of every customer who comes into your studio, whether that person buys or not. They have at least made the effort to visit and see what you do and have for sale. They are potential customers for sales in the future. Sometimes getting their names and addresses is as simple as asking them to sign the guest book. If your studio conveys a warm, homey atmosphere it is very easy. I have found, however, that it helps to have a reason for them to sign. For example, you may get their name and address by saying "I really appreciate you stopping by. We have special sales several times a year and I'd like to put you on our mailing list so that I can let you know about them. Not only do you save money but you get to look at all the new pieces before the general public does. Just write your name and address here and I'll take care of the rest."

You might use your mailing list to send out information about mail order sales from your studio. Experience shows that mail order sales work well with customers who have previously purchased from you at your studio, in contrast to using 'cold lists'.

□   PROMOTING SPECIAL EVENTS

To sell from your studio you must do something to get people to come to it. Look at what other retailers do to attract customers. You'll quickly find that they always give a specific reason for asking you to come, a January white sale, a pre-inventory sale, an assistant manager's sale, etc., etc. Think of what you can do. You might announce a kiln opening party, or a pre-Christmas showing for preferred customers, or an exhibition of another artist's work, or a Fall foliage celebration or any number of events. Be careful about having sales. It gives your studio a bad reputation and gives customers the impression that you carry inferior merchandise (otherwise why would you put it on sale)? Instead convey the image that the customer is going to experience a special event by coming to what you have planned.

□   ADVERTISE, ADVERTISE

If nobody knows where you are they will not come to see and buy. Therefore, you must let them know. The first thing you must do is produce a brochure describing what you do and where you are located. Take what ever time you need to develop an interesting brochure that successfully conveys your uniqueness. Then have a few thousand printed up and start sending them out. Where? Here are some must places:

1. The state tourist organization. Usually it is listed under state government offices. Call or write to obtain their policy for placing your brochures in tourist offices throughout the state. Sometimes they charge a fee, sometimes not. But it's vital that you get your brochure into their offices because millions of people visit them every year, thousands will pick up your brochure, and hundreds will visit your studio.

2. The local tourist organization. It may be a county or regional organization. For example, in Georgia we have two active organizations promoting tourism; one for the coastal area and one for the mountains. Contact the organization in your area and become a member. They are in business to help business owners in their area. If possible become active in the organization because the more exposure you get the better your sales. If a tourist is in another gallery or store and asks about galleries in the area you will get a referral.

3. The craft association(s) in the area. You may or may not have an active craft association in your region, but if you do you should join. The exposure will be good for you and you will have a number of craft enthusiasts who will know about you and your studio. There probably will not be any competition as most craft people do not sell from their studios on a full-time basis.

□ SELLING OTHER CRAFTSMEN'S WORK

Consider the possibility of selling the work of other craftsmen; work that complements yours. The decision is yours, but I think it is a good idea. People come to your studio to buy crafts, very often not knowing in advance what you have for sale or what they are looking for. The greater the variety, the better the chances you will make a sale. I sell to a number of studios and it works fine. The studio owner buys my work because it does not compete with his and sells well. He profits and so do I.

If you do decide to sell the work of other craftsmen, buy the work outright. Consignment creates more problems in bookkeeping than it's worth. If you are just getting started or are unsure of whether the work of a new craftsman will sell try consignment, but get out of it as soon as possible.

□ CHOOSING A LOCATION

The sad truth is no matter how charming your studio, no matter what a nice person you are or how much you love people, if your studio is in the wrong place you will fail. In the other marketing channels it doesn't make any differences where you make your crafts or what your studio looks like because you take your products to the customer. In direct studio sales the customer comes to you. If you make it too difficult for him he won't come. You have, in marketing terms, a space problem; there may be too much space between you and your customers.

There are several factors to consider in planning a location for your studio.

1. Customers: How many are there and how far away are they.
2. Appeal of the area: What would cause people to come to the area in which your shop is located?
3. Income level of your customers: Crafts are not a need item. You may have millions of customers within 50 miles of your studio but if they are all living hand-to-mouth they won't buy your work.

Let's go back to our earlier example of John and Glen LaRowe and see how they dealt with the location selection. The LaRowe's chose their site because it was in an area they loved, the mountains. They knew from the beginning that they wanted a single place, to live, work and sell from. When an old mill became available they immediately bought it. For years John worked in Atlanta, living in a small apartment during the week and spending the weekends at the mill studio. They chose the right spot because it was only a little more than an hour and a half away from Atlanta, a city with a population of 2,000,000, many of them affluent and well educated. In addition, their studio was located in a popular resort area with many recreational features year round. Affluent Atlantans come to the mountains to play the year round and stop at The Mark of the Potter. John tells me that business has increased every year since he has opened.

I strongly recommend that you conduct a market survey before you buy or rent a location for your studio. Choosing the right location for your studio is as vital as choosing the right craft fair to sell at. If you are depending on studio sales for your total income, selecting the correct location can mean the difference between success and failure. As the old real estate slogan goes, the three most important factors to consider in purchasing real estate are location, location and location. The same thing applies in selecting a studio site.

Obviously if you already have a studio you won't have the luxury of selecting the best location. In this case you must objectively analyze your situation. Advertising will help but it still may not be possible to generate enough sales from the studio. If not you'll need to develop other outlets as well, which is what most craftsmen do anyway. After all, the whole point of this book is to show you how to generate a marketing plan that works for you. It probably will not consist of just one marketing channel.

□ BUSINESS HOURS

Do you want to have customers come to your studio every hour that you are working? Are there times during the year that you should be open more hours than others? Some craftsmen open their studios just in the Summer months, leaving nine months to do their work without interruption. You will need to decide for yourself, keeping in mind the craftsman's age old dilemma of balancing sales with production. Or put another way, every hour you spend selling is an hour taken away from production. Every hour you spend talking with customers in your studio is an hour lost to production.

Here is a suggested schedule. Let's suppose that you sell from your studio and live upstairs. You know that you'll need some time away from the studio just to do errands, go to the doctor or dentist, have the car fixed, etc. You also know that weekends will be your busiest time. You plan to work from 8 a.m. to 5 p.m. every day so you work out the following schedule:

OPEN Weekdays 10:00 to 5:00
Saturdays 10:00 to 6:00
Sundays 1:00 to 5:00
Closed all day Wednesday

This will give you time in the morning to get set-up, run to the bank, etc., etc. You will need to adjust your hours depending on the customer flow. If there is no business in the morning at all, open at noon or 1:00. Use your judgment keeping in mind that you want to balance the sales-production ratio to maximize results for you.

□ LEGAL AND PROFESSIONAL MATTERS

I have until now intentionally avoided talking about taxes, business licenses, insurance and bookkeeping because they really are not marketing concerns. However, when you sell from your studio you subject yourself to a whole new set of rules and regulations. If you are aware of them and conform, you can concentrate on marketing your crafts. If you don't, you won't stay in business. Here are some things to think about.

Business License: Required for any business, usually obtained from your country government.

Health Inspection: Varied, depending on the type of business but give the health department a call, describe what you are doing and ask if they need to inspect your business.

Fire Safety: The fire department has a lot more power than many people realize. They can shut you down very quickly if they deem your business a fire hazard. Check it out with them before you open for business.

Zoning: If your studio is in a residential area you may not be allowed to sell from it unless you get a waiver from your neighbors.

Every county has specific laws. See what regulations apply to your business.

`   *Insurance:* Check with your insurance agent to see what coverage you need. Remember people who come into your studio can and will sue you if they are harmed while in your shop.

Tax Number: If your state has a sales tax you will be required to collect tax on every item you sell. In order to do that you must apply for, and sometimes pay a fee to get, a tax number so that you can collect taxes for the state.

All this may sound a little overwhelming but it really isn't. If you are just getting started it might be a good idea to talk to some of the other small business owners in the area to see what they had to do to open their businesses.

□   STUDIO

1. People come to your studio looking for an experience.
2. Location is crucial to your sales, the second consideration is location, the third is location.
3. Keep an accurate list of names and addresses of every person who comes by your studio.
4. Advertise all the time to keep your business in the minds of present and future customers.
5. Join local and regional craft associations so that you can develop personal contacts with other craftsmen.
6. Consider selling the work of fellow craftsmen in your studio. It will mean more sales and more customers.
7. Select a site that appeals to tourists.
8. Select a site that is close to population centers with people of above average incomes.
9. A market survey will tell you if the site you chose will support your business, before you take the risk of setting up your business.
10. Establish reasonable business hours but leave some free time for yourself.
11. Consult with professionals to make sure you have all the necessary permits, licenses, insurance, tax stamps, etc., etc., etc.
12. Consider alternative marketing channels for the slow months.

PART THREE

Wholesale Marketing Strategies

Chapter 10

Introduction to Wholesale Marketing Strategies

More and more craftsmen are finding wholesale marketing to be very profitable, and as interest in crafts continues to grow there will be additional markets available for quality crafts.

☐ ADVANTAGES

You can quickly build a reputation for quality if you select the right outlets. Selling in Neiman Marcus or Saks Fifth Avenue, for example, looks excellent on your resume and establishes you as a craftsman producing a quality product desired by affluent buyers. Further, wholesale buyers are always looking for something new. They don't go to every wholesale show but you can be sure that they check out the competition every chance they get. If your work is on display it could well mean on order from a competing buyer.

Selling costs are greatly reduced, as a rule. You still have to bear the expense of making the initial sales to the wholesale buyer but once the sale is made you should get additional orders with little effort on your part. I'm not suggesting that you will get further sales without any effort; you'll need to stay in touch with the buyers, but you won't have to spend the hours on sales demanded by the retail market.

The wholesale buyer does the most difficult job of selling to the first time buyer. All salesmen know that making the sale for the first time is the big hurdle. You'll see later why mail order sellers depend so much on repeat orders. Cold mailings to prospective buyers are considered good if they get a 2% response. Follow-up letters to established buyers often get a 20% response — ten times greater than the initial mailing.

Wholesale orders are generally larger. A wholesale buyer orders what she thinks will sell in a quantity that will satisfy customer demand. She is in fact buying for many rather than individually as is the case in the retail market.

☐ DISADVANTAGES

There really are only two: you get a lower price for your product and you sometimes have to wait a long time to get paid.

The standard discount in the crafts business is 50%. So, if you sell a craft piece at $20 retail you sell it at $10 wholesale. There are some wholesalers, department stores for example, that mark up the retail price even higher, sometimes as much as 200%, citing high overhead and marketing costs.

Pricing policies occasionally can create problems because some buyers may complain to you about different prices at different outlets. You should respond that your wholesale prices are the same for everyone. So the difference in retail price is in percentage of mark-up, over which you have no control.

The item you sell wholesale is exactly the same item you sell retail, costing you exactly the same for materials, labor and overhead. The only difference is that you receive only half the price at wholesale that you receive at retail. If that difference can be madeup by a reduction in selling costs then you have a winner. If not then you had better consider some other marketing channel.

Very often, especially when you are dealing with large volume wholesale buyers they will ask for terms, often 60 and sometimes 90 days. The reasons are obvious. The longer a buyer can put off paying you the longer he can use your money interest free. Banks do it all the time. Perhaps the best example of making use of other people's money is American Express. They built a multimillion dollar business selling travelers' checks. When you buy travelers' checks you pay cash, cash which American Express puts to work immediately. American Express even had the audacity recently to suggest that you put away any left-over travelers' checks to use in an emergency, should you ever need it. That's very considerate of them!

☐ TERMS

Earlier, in Chapter 4, we talked about basic business terms. I'd like to talk here about selling terms that you probably will encounter in the wholesale market. Wholesale buyers expect terms, which means they'll want to pay you later for what they have ordered. Offering attractive terms will increase your sales but you may not get paid. Here are some possible solutions:

No Minimum Initial Order, $100 Minimum Repeat Order
This approach has several advantages. First, it allows the wholesale buyer to test market your work in his store or gallery at a low investment. This will often make the difference between a sale and a no sale. It's officially called in marketing terms 'a low barrier to entry'. Plus, consider the fact that selling crafts in the wholesale market channels is still a relatively new phenomenon. As a newcomer, buyers are reluctant to take risks, so you have to convince them to try some-

thing new. If it only costs them a little money to try they will be much more willing to take a chance.

The $100 minimum repeat order protects you from being harassed by $10 and $15 orders. If your items did not sell well in the test he will not order anyway and if they did sell well he would want to order at least a $100 worth.

Cash for First Order, 30 Days Net on Repeat Orders

This arrangement requires that the buyer pay in full for the first order. If everything works out well (the check clears) the customer is assumed to have established a good credit rating and is offered 30 days net on all repeat orders. Payment is expected within 30 days; a late penalty of 1½% per month, 18% per year is assessed on all overdue accounts.

Credit Given for Approved Accounts

Ask the buyer for a list of at least three credit references. Call the references to learn if the customer pays his bills. Try to get the names of fellow craftsmen as references if you can. You want to know how well they pay craftsmen like yourself, not how well they pay the rent.

I learned this little trick from a friend who is in the industrial linen business. I was in his office one day when he received a call from a new customer. Obviously the customer on the other end asked for credit because my friend said "Sure we offer credit terms. Just send the names of at least three creditors and I'll check them out. Upon receipt of a favorable report I'll send out your order. Remember now, I don't want the names of your chemical suppliers; you need those to function. Send me the names of other people that you do business with."

When he got off the phone I asked him about what he said. His reply was "Any business has cash flow problems from time to time. When things get tight some things get paid and others don't. Because my product is not absolutely essential to him I want to know how he pays the bills of other 'nonessential accounts." It makes sense.

Pro-Forma or C.O.D. Accounts

Both arrangements work well for the craftsman and the buyer. The pro-forma account works this way. A buyer places an order with you. When you have completed the order and are ready to ship you call the buyer and inform him. Upon receipt of payment you ship the order.

C.O.D. is similar but is collected upon delivery of the order. The delivery person, UPS, trucker or post office collects the cost of the order plus shipping plus C.O.D. charges; keeps the C.O.D. charges and shipping costs for himself and sends you a check for the C.O.D. specified by you. The disadvantage of C.O.D. is the administrative charge but it is used frequently for first time accounts.

Net 60 Days

Not my favorite by any means, but sometimes necessary to make a sale. Larger accounts often ask for this as a matter of policy as it is a fairly standard practice. The reason is obvious: the larger buyer gets to keep the receipts from the sales of your work for 60 days before paying you.

The individual craftsman normally can't wait that long. If the buyer will order only if given the 60 days terms you might consider it, but try for 30 days. Also, check their credit and get references. Just because a buyer represents a major company doesn't mean that you will automatically get paid on time. There is a danger that you will be treated as the little fish in the pond and get paid only after all the big fishes have been fed.

Consignment

Not usually encountered in wholesale transactions but it still exists in sales to galleries. My advice is to not even mention it as a possibility. Gallery buyers will ask for it. It is up to you to decide whether the arrangement will benefit you or not.

What's Best

I believe that the following arrangement is best for most craftsmen: No minimum order initially; $100 minimum subsequent orders; pro-forma or C.O.D. for first orders; 30 days net for repeat orders; no consignment.

Order Fulfillment

I can guarantee that the fastest way to go out of business is to take orders and either not fill them or fill them improperly. The sad fact is that craftsmen still have the reputation of fly-by-night operators. In 99% of the cases this is not true but the image still exists. You can combat that personally by doing two things:

1. Fill all orders on time, exactly as specified.
2. Accept only those orders that you can reasonably fulfill.

Let's take a look at both in more detail. When you take an order it will be very specific, i.e., 27 red 48 blue 16 green and 124 white . . . . Make sure you fill it exactly. I recommend that you send a photo copy of the original order form with the shipment so the buyer can confirm immediately that his order has been correctly filled.

Be realistic about your production abilities. All of us dream of the time when we have so many orders that we can't fill them all. You cannot increase your production by ten times without making substantial changes in your work habits and organization. If you are willing and able to do so it's fine, but what if you're not? If you cannot fill an order, tell the buyer and don't take it! Put them on a waiting list and tell them that you will contact them as soon as you are able to accept new orders. They will respect you for such forthrightness and will wait, nine times out of ten.

□ PRICING

You already know how to calculate your real costs in making your pieces so you know what you have to get as a wholesale price to make a profit. Keep that figure in mind because you probably will be pressured to lower your prices by some wholesale buyers. I recommend that you don't lower your prices for any reason. You make labor intensive one-of-a-kind items and they cost you so much to make. Tell the buyer that your price is firm regardless of volume. If they need more profit margin they can either raise their retail price or cut down on their overhead.

□ FOLLOW-UP

It is your responsibility to stay in touch with the customer. Many craftsmen still believe that once an order is filled the store will order more when needed. That's not true. The buyer is not buying only from you but from many other craftsmen and often needs a gentle reminder that you are still around and in the crafts business.

When I started wholesaling my work I sat back waiting for the repeat orders to start coming in. Some did, but only a small percentage. After a couple of months I called on some accounts only to be criticized for not calling sooner. "We've been out of your work for three weeks. When you didn't call we figured that maybe you were not working anymore."

Keep in mind that while convincing the customer to buy the first time is much more difficult than it is later on, you should consider him to be a lifelong customer and that requires that you stay in touch.

The best way to stay in touch is with a descriptive brochure of your work. These should be given out at every contact with a wholesale buyer, whether at a wholesale buyer's show or at a gallery or shop. They need something to refer to be reminded of your work. Many times sales are made not at the time of initial contact but a week or month later when the customer needs a particular item and sees it in the brochure they had taken when they first met you.

When you add new items or have a price change, make it a point to update all your customers. They will reward your business-like attitude with repeat orders.

□ PROFESSIONAL IMAGE

When in Rome is appropriate here . . . . Different products and different wholesale outlets require different approaches. I'll describe what is best in each market channel a little later but for now keep in mind that you need to dress the part. If you are selling at a wholesale craft show where all the buyers are dressed to the hilt and you're in your jeans you have set up an unnecessary barrier between yourself and the buyer.

☐ EXCLUSIVE RIGHTS

Some wholesale buyers will ask for exclusive rights to be the only outlet for your work in their particular geographical area. Before you agree to an exclusive make sure that it is in your best interest. I suggest you give it a trial period of say, six months to determine how sales are. If they are good and the outlet is not in your immediate area then it is probably a good idea to agree to an exclusive.

Always make sure that an exclusive is the best deal for you. If there are a number of excellent outlets for your work in the local area you would be unwise to accept an exclusive with one shop or gallery as you would lose the sales from others.

☐ MARKET DISTRIBUTION

Financial advisors recommend mutual funds to investors because they diversify their stock holding, thus minimizing the chances of an overwhelming loss if a particular stock begins to fall dramatically. The same holds true in selecting retail outlets for your work. The rule of thumb is commit no more than 20% of your production to any one outlet. Why? Because of the potential for significant loss should that outlet go out of business.

A true story to illustrate what can happen: A potter in the Southeast had an exclusive with a contemporary home furnishing store with outlets throughout the South. They purchased everything he produced and everyone was happy. Then the chain decided to change its marketing strategy and did away with crafts. The potter was left with no outlets and no income. He fought back, eventually establishing new accounts. He is doing well today but has learned a hard lesson.

Chapter 11

Marketing Strategies: Selling to Shops and Galleries

☐ ENTERING THE MARKET

It's your career and your business, so you should select the shops and galleries that fit your image. This is fairly easy to do locally because you can visit each gallery and see for yourself whether or not you want to associate with them. If you like what you see, make plans with the owner to present your work.

Proceed locally by making a list of galleries in your area that you want to approach. If there are two galleries very close together, select the one which you think best fits your image and approach it first. If they accept your work, do not contact the other gallery. One of the surest ways to create bad feelings is by saturating a particular area with your work.

Proceed slowly! Make sure that you can meet the needs of one gallery before you expand into others. If a gallery experiences difficulty getting your work time after time, it will look elsewhere. Keep your market channels supplied and happy.

When you are ready to select galleries out of town, the best approach is a personal visit. For economic reasons, however, a personal visit is not always possible, but it still remains the preferred approach.

State craft organizations often have lists of galleries looking for craftspeople. Craft magazines publish lists of shops and galleries seeking craftspeople. One of the best and most current is found in *The Crafts Report*. Each issue carries a Crafts Wanted section. A typical listing reads:
    The Craft Shed
    126 Ocean Lane
    Bath, ME 04530
    Contact: Bruce Stein (618) 414-3382
    All Crafts: especially pottery, baskets, soft goods, jewelry, cards. Retail to $800; purchase (50%) and consignment (60%). Submit slides, price list, SASE.

The *Quality Crafts Report* has a similar listing, but may not come out frequently enough to be useful. You might also try *The Craftsworker's Market*. The book is no longer in print, but you can borrow a copy from your library or through a friend. The book lists 3,200 outlets selling crafts, some of which may no longer be in business. I'd protect myself by sending a postcard inquiring whether or not they are looking for new craftspeople. If they say yes, you know they are still in business.

It is essential that I clear the air about what it's really like approaching a gallery to sell your work. If you're apprehensive about contacting gallery owners, join the crowd. Many craftspeople are nervous about approaching galleries because they are afraid of being turned down. That does happen, but the truth is that galleries are always looking for new craftspeople and new work. The chances of your work being accepted are greater than being rejected if you do your homework before you contact the gallery.

The Personal Contact

This is always the best approach, but before you contact any gallery, do some research and identify the galleries which feature your type of craft. There are some galleries with which you won't want to be associated and some galleries that won't want to be associated with you.

I use the advice call approach when I contact a shop or gallery and have *never* been turned down for an appointment. Sure, there were times when galleries didn't want my work, but then I really didn't go to the gallery to sell my work anyway, only to get some advice. Here's how the advice call works.

The first thing you must do is get the owner's name. If you have visited the shop in advance of making an appointment, you should have already obtained the owner's name. If you haven't, use this technique: call the gallery and say, "I'd like to speak to the owner, please." In most cases the owner will answer the phone because most galleries are small. Then say, "Hello, I'm interested in hand-made leather items. Do you carry them?" If the answer is yes, then say, "Great, I'll be on by. Are you there every day? I'd like to meet with you personally. Your name was?"

A few days later, call to set up an appointment. It's important that you use the owner's name when you call as you want to give the impression that you know something about him and the shop. (You probably do anyway.)

Here's the approach I use. I call saying, "Is Ms. Smith in?" When she comes to the phone, I say, "Ms. Smith, my name is Brian Jefferson. I'm a leather craftsman and have heard from many people that you have an excellent selection in your gallery. I'm in a position now to supply a quality gallery such as yours and would like to come by and get your opinion on the sales potential of my work. I realize that your schedule is hectic at times, so I would be willing to come by at a time that is convenient for you. Which is better, mornings or after-noons?"

This works every single time and puts you and the owner in a relaxed position because you are not asking the owner to buy your wares, only for an opinion. Nine times out of ten, you'll be asked to leave some of your samples to see how they sell. If they sell well you have established a new gallery association. If you are not asked to leave some samples, thank the owner for her time and say, "I understand that my work doesn't fit your marketing plan at this particular time. Perhaps you could suggest the names of some other galleries that might be interested in carrying my work." When the owner suggests another gallery or two make sure that you get the names of the owner(s).

Call them and say, "Hi, my name is Brian Jefferson. I'm a leather worker and Ms. White of the Butterfly Gallery suggested that I call because she felt that my work would appeal to your customers. I'd like to get your opinion; can I show you my work some time this week? What time is best for you?"

Always use what personal contact you have. Do it all the time. One gallery turned me down after I had shown my work. That was no problem because it was an advice call. I asked her if she had any other galleries she might suggest. She did, so I called, used her name, and got an appointment in an hour to meet with the owner. I sold my complete sample kit and have been selling to her ever since.

If you make an advice call over the phone and the gallery owner for some reason is not in the market for additional crafts, simply say, "I understand that. Let me send you my card and a few slides. If you do see a need for my work in the future, or know of another gallery that might be interested, I'd appreciate it if you would contact me. Thanks for your time."

When you arrive for your advice appointment, be sure that you present the right image. Don't wear a suit or a formal dress. You are a craftsperson who had dedicated your life to making things. Dress neatly, but casually. Dress as though you were going for an appointment with another professional — a doctor, dentist or accountant. Be yourself, but be neat and clean. I've seen some craftspeople who look like they've just climbed out of the clay pit or the wood pile. That's okay for the studio, but not for sales calls. Concern for your appearance reflects the fact that you are concerned about your crafts.

Gallery Contacts Through the Mail

How you dress is not important when you contact galleries through the mail, but your mail package is. The impression your envelope, slides, resume, etc., etc. give are all vitally important. Here are the essential ingredients:

1. A personal letter. If you are sending out lots of letters to galleries you can have them autotyped. This is a computerized typing process that not only individually types each letter, but also inserts the correct inside address. Because each letter is individually typed the gallery receives a personal letter from

you. It can save you a lot of time and money. The reason for all this is to give the gallery the impression that you are giving them your individual attention. If possible, use your own letterhead.

Your letter should include the reasons you are writing to them and a brief explanation of how you can be of service to them. When galleries are approached by out-of-state craftspeople, they want the answers to several questions:

> Is this craftsman's work quality work?
> Is this craftsman reliable (will orders be delivered on time)?
> Is this craftsman's work unique (galleries can get all the
> 'standard' craft items from local sources)?
> Does the work sell?

Obviously, you could state in your letter that "I do quality work, am reliable, do unique work and my items sell," but there is a better way! Here is a sample letter. You can make changes to personalize it any way you want, but note that it very nicely addresses the four points listed above.

Ms. Rose Pollie, Owner
Frog Hollow Gallery
2967 Ocean Way
Jacksonville, FL   01862

Dear Ms. Pollie:

I am writing in response to your ad in the Crafts Wanted section of the Crafts Report. I have been a craftsman for the past ten years and maintain active accounts with several fine galleries in the southeast. The names and addresses of these galleries can be supplied to you if you wish to check my references.

During the past two years I have been selling, on a selective basis, to quality galleries in several other parts of the country. At the present time I do not have a gallery association in your area and am forwarding my materials to explore the possibility of being represented by your gallery.

The enclosed vita outlines my professional background and exhibition record. Currently I produce a range of twenty different items. The four slides I have enclosed represent the quality of my work. A complete price list is included which lists all the items currently produced.

Should you be interested in seeing samples of my work, I would be willing to ship a sample order of any amount. Repeat orders must be for a minimum of $100.

Obviously, I have not had the opportunity to visit your gallery personally, so I don't know exactly the type of work you are seeking. If my work does not fit the image you are developing, perhaps you could suggest the name or names of other galleries in your area that would be interested in my craft items.

I've enclosed a SASE for your convenience, and would appreciate the return of the slides with your response.

Thank you for your consideration.

Sincerely,

2. Send slides. I send four in plastic slide holders. This protects them and makes them easy to look at. By all means write on the front of the slide frame what the item is, the medium and the dimensions.

3. Send a resume of your education, exhibition experience and special awards. If this is a new market channel for you don't say anything, but let your work speak for itself. When you have been accepted by a few galleries you can start your list.

It's a good idea to design your resume or vita (the same thing) to appeal to the market channel you are working on. Here is the vita I use when I send to galleries out of town. Notice that it simplifies my educational background and exhibition record, but emphasizes the galleries I am associated with. Use one vita for entering juried shows, another for craft fairs, another for galleries, etc., etc.

```
                    Professional Profile

Personal Data:
                Brian T. Jefferson
                4170 Durham Circle
                Stone Mountain, Georgia
                404-292-2665

Educational Background:
                Massachusetts College of Art    B.S.   1964
                Pennsylvania State University   M.Ed.  1967
                Pennsylvania State University   D.Ed.  1971

Exhibitions:
                Work shown in over forty national and inter-
                    national shows

Current Gallery Associations:

Mark of the Potter      Clarksville, Georgia
Rainblue Gallery        Roswell, Georgia
Hyatt Regency Gallery   Atlanta, Georgia
Charlie's Gallery       Buckhead, Georgia
Clayton House Gallery   Stone Mountain, Georgia
E.S.P. Gallery          Rockport, Massachusetts
The Mole Hole           Sarasota, Florida
Glynn Art Galleries     St. Simon's Island, Georgia
A Touch of Glass        Decatur, Georgia
Gallery Five            Roswell, Georgia
Collector's Cove        Atlanta, Georgia
Clapper Rail            St. Simon's Island, Georgia

Professional Organizations:
                American Crafts Council
                Georgia Art Education Association
                National Education Association
```

4. Send a business card. Many galleries will not be in a position to buy upon receipt of your letter, but may want to order in the future. A business card gives them an instant reference should they want to contact you.
5. Send a self-addressed, stamped envelope (SASE). This is always a good business practice, but it is absolutely essential if you are doing the soliciting. No gallery is under any obligation to return your slides or any other material if you fail to enclose a SASE.
6. Send a current price list and order blank. This makes it a lot easier for a shop to order. In addition, by photocopying their order when you fill it, the order acts as a shipping copy readily matched to what they ordered.

You can expect about a 10% response from your gallery contacts. If you want to be handled by ten different galleries, you'll need to contact at least a hundred. It will take time, but the rewards will be worth it.

One of the advantages of including a SASE is that the galleries will return the slides and you can send them out to other galleries and other galleries and other galleries. When you prepare your slide package, have ten duplicate sets made to illustrate each type of piece you do. Then you'll have ten complete sets of slides that you can rotate between galleries. Do the same thing when you design new pieces, so your slide packages are always up to date.

What do you do if you want to contact a gallery that you know nothing about plus you have no idea if they are looking for new craftspeople or not? Here's a sample letter that I use with some success. Admittedly it is not nearly as successful as the letters and materials I send to galleries that I know want work. The response to this type of letter is about 2% and of those responding, only about 10% place an order. You decide for yourself if you think it's worth it.

Note that this approach differs from the previous in the following ways:
1. The initial mailing contains a letter and a stamped, self-addressed postcard. All the gallery owner has to do is drop the postcard in the mail.
2. The slides, SASE and other materials are sent to the people returning the postcard. Any other approach is too costly.

Dear

I produce a series of hand built and wheel thrown ceramic pieces
that I currently wholesale to galleries and gift shops from
Massachusetts to Florida. It took fifteen years of trial and
tribulation to develop a line that meets my expressive needs and
is highly saleable as well, but I think I have done it.

Here's my proposition. I'd like to send you a brochure and slides
of my work, and would appreciate it if you would take a few minutes to
see if it fits into your gallery's image. Whatever your decision is,
I'd really appreciate an honest reaction to my work in relation to
the needs of your gallery. I'm pretty thick-skinned, so be as honest
as you like.

I realize that an item that sells well in one gallery may be a slow
mover in another. For example, some of my best selling items are press
molded porcelain and stoneware birds that I produce in four sizes and
in three different glaze effects. One shop in Georgia has great results
with the small birds, but less with the largest bird. In another instance
I tripled my sales on one item because I listened when a gallery director
said, "You know, these would sell much better if you did them in blue."

I want to make a living doing what I enjoy and am asking you to help
me do it. It will take a few minutes of your time, but I think you
will find it profitable. If you are at all interested, return the
card and I'll send the brochure and slides out to you. If you don't
like them (I'm not perfect) send them back (at my expense), and that's
the last you will hear from me.

Just in case you like what you see, but are still not convinced,
I've enclosed a list of the galleries that currently carry my work.
Feel free to contact them if you like.

Have a nice day!

Brian Jefferson

BTJ:sls

□   MARKETING STRATEGIES

Once you have made contact with a gallery and they have placed an order with you, you have overcome the most difficult hurdle, but it is no time to sit back and relax. Now is the time to develop and enhance your business relationship. Keep in mind that the gallery agreed to represent you because they felt your work satisfied at least one of their needs (sales). If you continue to satisfy that need, you'll continue to do business. If you can identify and satisfy additional needs, your business will grow.

Make it a habit to contact your gallery connections once every month or so. Don't deliver your order and wait for them to contact you when they need more. That's not the way! Gallery owners are busy and they know that craftspeople are busy, too. Do them the courtesy of calling them and saying, "Hi, I'm just checking in to see if you need anything and to see how those new samples are doing, etc., etc."

When you do try a new design, make it clear that you'll happily replace the new objects at no cost to the gallery if they do not sell. This is particularly worthwhile when dealing with established gallery accounts. The gallery is as interested as you are in making money by selling quality crafts. They are willing to experiment to see if a new product does sell. If it does, both parties benefit. If it doesn't, nobody has lost too much.

Every person who walks into a gallery exhibiting your work is a potential customer. There is a delicate balance between keeping your own integrity and making crafts that will sell. I don't think there is anything wrong with modifying your designs to increase sales. In fact if you are not willing to respond to the demands of the customers, your chances of having a successful crafts business are very slim indeed.

Listen to the gallery owner. He or she is your best friend. The owner is there when people buy or reject your work. Consequently, you learn a great deal about customers' reactions to your work from him. If the gallery owner reports that people are asking whether your woven placemats come in other colors, you should expand your color range. If your spoon jars are too large, make them smaller. If your jewelry sells best in sets, display them that way.

Establish the reputation of a professional who is willing to explore new possibilities and new designs. The gallery owner will contact you with requests for new products in your area. If you don't feel it's appropriate for you, simply say that you don't have time for that at the present, and suggest someone else, if you can!

□   HOW TO PROMOTE YOUR WORK

Assuming that both you and the gallery are profiting from the arrangement, there is a lot that you can do to help publicize your work.

The first thing you can do is produce a card or brochure that tells people about your work. People want to know who made the work they are buying and how it was made. The example below is a brochure used by Margaret Agner. Because Margaret uses an unusual process, her brochure becomes even more important, serving as a sales tool and an educational tool at the same time.

You might want to work with a gallery to have an opening once or twice a year. A number of potters have a kiln opening twice a year. They send special invitations to all their good customers inviting them to their studio for an exclusive viewing. It takes on the feeling of a party if wine, cheese and hors d'oeuvres are served. See if you can do the same thing with your gallery connections. You and the gallery can split the expense of sending out invitations, serving champagne and share the profits from sales.

Demonstrate at some of the galleries where your work is shown. One crafts shop in a state park has high tourist traffic. They have craftspeople demonstrating every weekend during the summer season. It's a great crowd pleaser and increases sales dramatically.

Send news releases to all the local and regional publications. Every newspaper has an arts section and they are always looking for news about what's happening in the arts.

□ COMPETITION

Competition can be good for you if you take advantage of it. It can be disastrous if you fail to keep up with what others are doing.

Competition from other craftspeople keeps you on your toes and the better your product becomes, the more you will be able to charge for it because you are judged by the company you keep (or at least your craft is). You can expect to sell crafts within a certain price range at a mall show. You can also reasonably expect to sell at a much higher price if your work is shown in a prestigious gallery. Remember, always match your product and your market.

Each gallery develops its own clientele. After they have been in business for a few years they carefully select the artists they represent because their work appeals to the gallery's customers. Competition from other craftspeople may stimulate you to expand your horizons to attract customers in galleries that you are not now in.

Some galleries are highly specialized which can help build your reputation as well. Suppose you sell to a shop that has the work of over fifty other potters. Your sales will be good if your work is not like any other potter in the gallery and the gallery has a reputation for carrying the work of quality potters so the gallery attracts people interested in buying ceramics.

It is important that you establish a reputation for quality. If you find that your expensive work is not selling well enough to keep you solvent you might produce some lower cost items but sell them to other galleries. It's not a good idea to combine high and low priced items in the same studio.

Your sales will improve if you have an area in the display space set aside exclusively for your work. A gallery will do this if your work is selling well and if you keep them well supplied. Every gallery has at least five or six craftspeople who they feature by having a special display of their work. If you're not one of them, try to figure out why. If it's because your work is not selling, find out why. When your sales do reach a respectable level, work out an arrangement with the gallery owner to have a space of your own.

Needless to say, you should always be working to improve your work so that you can compete effectively with other craftspeople in the same gallery. As a potter, I'm always looking for new clays, glazes, designs, techniques, etc. Whenever I deliver an order, I always look around and make a point to talk with the owner about how people are responding to my work. I listen carefully and try some of the suggestions on the next batch of pots. It pays off because my work is improved by dispassionate, but genuine, criticism and I'm excited because there are always new challenges and new ideas to try.

The more information you have about how customers react to your work the better your sales will be. Remember that you will always be in competition with other craftsmen, and that craft buyers are discriminating shoppers. If you have been in the business for a long time your name will be recognized and will help generate sales. However, your work must still be competitive. You need to know what other craftsmen are doing and how your work compares. In order to do that I suggest a:

□ COMPETITORS POSITIONING REPORT

Name of Business _____

Initial Impression _____

Impressions After Survey_____

_____

Competitor's Positioning Theme_____

_____

Effective Marketing Strategies _____

_____

Ineffective Marketing Strategies _____

_____

Price Quality Assessment_____

What you are looking for is a hole in the marketplace. If ten other craftsmen making stained glass are exhibited in this particular gallery you'll need to define what it is that is unique about your stained glass. If you are unable to do so the gallery owner will not have a need for your work because the customer already has a choice.

This type of analysis is relatively easy to do by visiting shops in your immediate location, but much more difficult if you are selling to galleries out of your geographical area. You will find that doing several competitors' positioning reports will clarify what is unique about your work. When you do contact out-of-state galleries you can use positioning surveys to say to the gallery owner "I am a stained glass craftsman specializing in architectural scale designs. I feel my work is unique because . . . ."

Positioning is something that every business does all the time. Get into the habit of analyzing and promoting the uniqueness of your work all the time.

☐ PRICING

The gallery owner knows what price range sells best and what other craftsmen are getting for their work. People comparison shop and they buy what *they consider* to be the best value.

Remember that just as you have positioned your product in the marketplace the gallery you sell to has also positioned itself. Its position may be "The Largest Selection of Hand-Crafted Pottery in the Southeast," or "Handmade by Mountain Folks," or "Fine Crafts for the Collector." Each projects an image and a price-set. A person visiting a shop catering to the craft collector expects to find one-of-a-kind, high priced crafts whereas a customer may frequent another gallery because, "It's the perfect place to get an unusual gift for $10 − $15."

Pricing is a sensitive issue. Frequently by making a minor change in the product, you can change the customer's image and, therefore, his willingness to pay your price. Simple things like signing the piece, attaching an explanatory tag or brochure, making it larger, smaller, packing it in a box, framing it, etc., etc. can help your sales.

☐ MARKET SUITABILITY

There's a long simmering debate among craftspeople about whether it's worth it to sell to galleries. The final decision is up to you, but I know many craftspeople who sell to galleries and do very well financially.

Admittedly, the profit is not as high when you sell wholesale, but as discussed earlier, there are other expenses that you are spared. Good accounting practices will tell you whether it is worthwhile for you or not. If you find it isn't profitable initially, figure out why and develop a new product line or marketing strategy.

The whole crafts marketing business is one of change. Galleries come and go, or change their priorities. Some of the galleries that were profitable a few years ago may not be today. Sometimes it is caused because craft tastes have changed; other times because the gallery has changed.

Remember that if you cannot make a profit selling wholesale you shouldn't do it, particularly if you have investigated all the possibilities in a specific market area. Making crafts is a highly individual process and the marketing of them is also. Find the right fit for you. It may be that selling to shops and galleries is just right for you, but it might be that it isn't and that other market channels are more suitable.

The Wholesale Market Survey

Name of Outlet _____

Address _____

City _____ State _____ ZIP _____

Phone _____ Business Hours _____

Buyer _____

Outlet Profile _____

_____

Date of First Sale _____ Total Sales _____

1st Year Sales _____ 2nd Year Sales _____

    Type _____   Type _____

    _____   _____

    _____   _____

    _____   _____

3rd Year Sales _____ 4th Year Sales _____

    Type _____   Type _____

    _____   _____

    _____   _____

    _____   _____

Items Requested _____

_____

Personal Data on Buyer _____

_____

Additional Comments _____

_____

_____

_____

☐ PLANNING FUTURE SALES

You already know how important keeping touch with your accounts is. The best way of doing so is by keeping accurate records so that you know what sells well at each outlet. Use a form to record the sales for each gallery or shop that you sell to. It's similar to the one I recommend for the Craft Fair and Mall Show only it's designed for the wholesale market. I call it:

☐ THE WHOLESALE MARKET SURVEY

This report should be on hand for every outlet that you sell to. Fill in as much of it as you can. If the owner mentioned to you that he would like a wider range of items from you jot that down in the comments. If you visit the shop and see a need for a particular item, list that under ideas for the future. Feel free to expand the Wholesale Market Survey to include any information you might want to have for your marketing plan.

☐ LEGAL OBLIGATIONS

In all my years in the crafts business, I have never signed a contract with a gallery. All transactions have been done on faith. Virtually all the craftspeople and gallery owners have told me that they work the same way. You do have moral and professional obligations when you work with a gallery, but they could not be called legal in the strict sense of the word.

Here's the way most craftspeople work. A gallery agrees to handle their work and submits an order. The craftsperson fills the order, delivers it and gets paid. When the gallery needs more, another order is submitted and the craftsperson fills it. It sounds simple and it is. You are producing a product and someone else is buying it. There are all kinds of assumed agreements in such a transaction, but few are spelled out.

It is an excellent idea to have a receipt of your order signed by the gallery owner when you deliver since some galleries don't pay upon receipt and you may need some evidence that your order was received. Otherwise you may have trouble collecting.

If you sell on consignment, a contract between the artist and the gallery is absolutely essential. If should include a list (in detail) of all the works left on consignment the price of each, a statement of ownership, the percentage due the artist and the gallery upon sale of a piece and how long the items will be displayed. Here is a sample:

It is hereby agreed between (artist) _____
(address) _____ :
and (dealer)_____
(address) _____ :
that the dealer shall exhibit the artist's work at the dealer's premises
under the following conditions.

1. The works consigned are listed and priced at retail on the attached list. The consigned works are the property of the artist and shall remain so until either they are sold or returned to the artist.
2. The works listed shall be exhibited by the dealer for a period not to exceed _____ days. At the end of that time, the artist and the dealer shall renegotiate this contract. The artist may individually remove work providing five days prior written notice has been given.
3. The dealer will pay the artist _____% of the retail sales price on any works sold. Notice of all sales, including the name and address of purchaser, will be given to the artist at the end of each month and payment of all moneys due shall be made not more than 30 days after the receipt of payment by the dealer.
4. During the time of this agreement the dealer shall insure the artist's work to an amount equal to the artist's portion of the retail sales price.
5. During the term of this agreement, the dealer will exclusively represent the artist in this particular geographical area.

Artist	Dealer

Date	Date

There are many variations of the contract and each gallery will probably have its own version. Make sure you understand the contract before you sign and make sure that the contract addresses the issues listed in the sample above. These are minimum requirements; other contracts may be more detailed. See Appendix D.

□   GETTING OUT

When you decide to get out of gallery sales you need to inform the galleries. I prefer a phone call. Tell them honestly why you will no longer sell to them and thank them for their support. If it is just a temporary moratorium on wholesale selling, tell them that also. It creates good will and maintains a professional relationship, allowing you to return to this market channel when you desire.

☐ SHOP AND GALLERY MARKET REVIEW

1. Make sure you can meet the demands of one gallery before you expand to two, or three or more.
2. Approach gallery and shop owners personally whenever possible.
3. Use the advice call approach to make initial contacts.
4. When contacting galleries by mail your mail package must look professional.
5. Always include a S.A.S.E. when you are initiating the contact.
6. Stay in touch with your shops and galleries; it means additional sales
7. Work with galleries to promote your work
8. Keep in touch with what your competition is doing so you can maintain your position in the marketplace.
9. Keep track of your pricing. If you cannot afford to sell at wholesale, don't.
10. Nobody has made a product that appeals to everyone. Choose the shops and galleries that fit your craft style.
11. Avoid consignment whenever possible. Use it to stimulate new sales outlets but switch to outright selling as soon as sales warrant.
12. If you do leave the market, contact all your accounts and tell them. You may want to re-enter at a later time.

Chapter 12

Market Profile: Selling to Wholesale Craft Shows

More and more craftsmen are finding it profitable to display their crafts at some of the wholesale craft events held throughout the country. Normally, the wholesale buyers market is held in conjunction with a crafts fair that is open to the public. However, there are some wholesale only shows. The wholesale days (only open to the trade) come before the public is allowed in and offer gallery, department store, gift shop, and other volume buyers an opportunity to view the crafts in a leisurely way, talk with the craftspeople and make their selections without being bothered by large crowds. In most cases the wholesale buyer places an order for crafts to be delivered on a specific date so that the craftspeople will still have a full booth when the general public is allowed in; a most important consideration.

□   ENTERING THE MARKET

There are several national wholesale crafts markets considered to be the best in the country because they are professionally run and are well attended. Five are run by American Craft Enterprises, Inc., P.O. Box 10, New Paltz, New York 12561; phone: 914-255-0039. They are The Fair At Baltimore, Dallas, Springfield, Newport and San Francisco. Information on any or all shows can be obtained by contacting American Craft Enterprises, Inc.

There are excellent regional shows held in all parts of the country. The sponsors of the shows are too numerous to mention here but try: New England Buyer's Marketplace, One Faneuil Hall Marketplace, Boston, Massachusetts, 02109 and American Crafts Salons, Sugarloaf, New York 10981. Your best source of information is one of the crafts marketing publications such as the *Crafts Report, The Quality Crafts Market* or *Sunshine Artists.*

The competition for the best wholesale shows is fierce. When a show builds an outstanding reputation, excellent craftsmen naturally want to exhibit their work in it. Some shows receive two to four times the number of applications they can accommodate. Competition has become so keen that one enterprising promoter sponsored a wholesale only show timed to coincide with the wholesale days of The Fair at Baltimore. The new show, called the Baltimore Buyers' Market, was held only three blocks from the established show and attracted 1200 buyers. The trend is clear and more shows will develop to meet demand. Be careful in choosing the ones you'll attend. Remember, though, it doesn't make any difference if you were the first exhibitor they ever had and have been exhibiting every year for the last seven years, your application will be judged on the same basis as every other craftsperson.

Now, here's the sleeper. There is evidence that craftspeople who have a record of established accounts with wholesale buyers will get preferential treatment. Why? Because show promoters want to attract buyers and buyers will come if they know the craftspeople exhibiting there are familiar with and can handle accounts with wholesale buyers. It makes sense. Naturally if two exhibitors have equal wholesale experience and one's work is of a higher quality than the other, one must assume that the judges will select the higher quality work.

I trust that you are getting the message in every crafts marketing channel that experience counts. It's difficult to break in sometimes but the more exposure you get the easier it becomes. If you are entering a new market don't give up before you really see if this is a potential profit area for you.

There is no question in my mind that tailoring your marketing approach to each individual marketing area is vital. When you apply to a wholesale crafts fair it is well worth your time to submit a list of your accounts and experience in the wholesale market. You might list the names and addresses of your present accounts, number of times they have reordered, the shows you have participated in and anything else you can think of that will demonstrate your experience in this area.

You should be aware that in some cases the sponsors of the show act as the jury or jury committee. They will select what they think is best but it may not coincide with your standard. Your best bet, regardless of the selection committee or selection process, is to present yourself in the best professional image and by all means tailor your presentation just for the wholesale market; it will increase your chances of acceptance.

Take a look at the materials used by the Atlanta Market Center for its Southeastern Craft Show '83.

The Show Announcement

This was sent to craftspeople and craft organizations throughout the southeast. When the craftspeople wrote back asking for more information they were sent the following:

The Welcoming Letter

A letter describing the show, booth fees and other details. Note that the letter calls attention to the fact that the Southeastern Craft

Show sponsors will be providing special services to assist the individual craftsperson enter what is probably a new market for him.

Application for Exhibit Space
Along with the welcome letter the craftsperson receives an application. Note that by signing this document you are agreeing to all the rules and regulations specified in the contract.

Basic Terms and Conditions
This one is quite typical. I draw your attention to item 7, *The Directory*. This is an important sales tool which may result in additional sales for you after the show is over.

Exhibit Space Map
This is a nice added plus. It allows the craftsperson the opportunity to select the space he or she wants. It gives people an incentive to apply early to get the booth they want.

Your booth fee insures that you have reserved that booth for the length of the show. Should an emergency arise which prevents attendance prior to the show you may get a refund of part of your booth rental fee. It all depends on how far ahead of time you notify the committee of your of your problem and their policies. The contract will state the refund policy.

SOUTHEASTERN CRAFT SHOW '83
March 12 - 15, 1983

The Southeastern Craft show offers exhibitors two hard-to-find advantages — a quality controlled exhibition of handicrafts and a well established retail buyer base. Adding an additional dimension, the Atlanta Market Center has drawn retail buyers from all over the southeast for 20 years. Criteria for entrance to the show insure a better exhibit with true craft and artisan merchandise. The show encourages on-site exhibitor demonstrations, which will enhance the atmosphere of creativity.

The show allows exhibitors to actually tap two potential buying markets:

1. **Wholesale.** The first three days of market attract thousands of retailers who regularly shop the Atlanta Market Center's Gift Show.
   Consider the advantages of selling wholesale in our Market Center.
   - **Sell in quantity rather than on a single item basis.**
   - **Broaden your customer base of wholesale buyers.**
   - **Benefit from well-promoted advertising program through direct mail and trade publications.**

2. **Retail.** On Tuesday, the show opens to the public.

To Qualify for Exhibit Space:

- The artisan or manufacturer will be present during the show.

- Craftsmen should possess the ability to produce work of both the quality and quantity necessary to fill wholesale orders.

- All crafts will be original and hand-made. No commercial mold or kit produced items will be shown.

- Potential exhibitors will submit slides or a detailed description of their craft(s).

Exhibitor Information

SPACE RATE
$300.00 per/ 9x12 booth

Space Rental Includes

1. Show site freight handling — receive at dock, deliver to booth space, store empty cartons, return cartons and reload for outbound.
2. Metal pegboard backwall of booth.
3. Side drape 36" high.
4. 18' of tables with plastic covering on tops.
5. One (1) light bar with three adjustable flood lights and drop cord (120V).
6. Waste basket and ashtrays.
7. Booth identification sign.
8. Market directory listing.
9. Directory of buyer provided following show.

An Exhibitor Bonus

Your show package includes a free workshop directed exclusively to the craft exhibitor. Held March 11, Friday, 3:00 - 5:00 p.m., this seminar will offer tips on wholesale marketing, discussing defining a target market, sales contracts, inventory and production schedules.

Show Dates and Hours

EXHIBITOR MOVE-IN
Thursday March 10, 1983 12:00 noon - 6:00 p.m.
Friday March 11, 1983 8:00 a.m. - until completion

SHOW HOURS
Saturday   March 12, 1983   9:00 a.m. - 6:00 p.m.
Sunday   March 13, 1983   9:00 a.m. - 6:00 p.m.
Monday   March 14, 1983   9:00 a.m. - 6:00 p.m.
Tuesday   March 15, 1983   9:00 a.m. - 12:00 p.m.
(Last day open to the public 12:00 noon - 8:00 p.m.)

EXHIBITOR MOVE-OUT
Wednesday March 16, 1983   8:00 a.m. - 12 noon

Discount Hotels/Airfares
For discount hotel reservations (from $35) call 1-800-241-6405; in Georgia, 1-800-282-0456. For discount Eastern air fare (30% off with no restrictions) call 1-800-327-1295; in Florida, 1-800-432-1217.

For additional information:
John Rosenberg
Atlanta Market Center
240 Peachtree Street
Atlanta, Ga. 30043
(404) 658-5616

ATLANTA MARKET CENTER
March 12 - 15, 1983

**Atlanta
Market
Center**

**Atlanta
Apparel Mart**

**Atlanta
Merchandise Mart**

**Atlanta Decorative
Arts Center**

December 10, 1982

Dear Craft Person:

Enclosed you will find detailed information concerning Southeastern Craft Show 83'. Please read over carefully and return to us slides or photographs of your work. The response for the show has been very strong so the sooner your work is reviewed the better your chances are of securing exhibit space. We are looking forward to this years new addition to the Gift Market and will be promoting such extras as:

1.) A free workshop directed to the craft exhibitor.
2.) On site demonstrations
3.) Seminars directed at buyers on the importance of having crafts in a retail store

Upon receipt of your slides/photos, and application, we will let you know of your status by mail or phone. We will then assign to qualifying applicants their booth space, send you additional information, and invo you for the $300.00. If you are interested in more than one booth spac it is advisable that you let us know the number of booths you will need Once again thank you for your interest in Southeastern Craft Show '83. If you have any further questions please call or write.

Best regards,

John Rosenberg

John Rosenberg
Craft Show Manager

JR/ae

enclosure   Atlanta Market Center
                 240 Peachtree Street
                 Suite 2200
                 Atlanta, Georgia   30043
                 (404) 658-5616

APPLICATION FOR EXHIBIT SPACE
SOUTHEASTERN CRAFT SHOW '83
Atlanta Market Center

WE HEREBY APPLY FOR EXHIBIT SPACE IN SOUTHEASTERN CRAFT SHOW '83. WE AGREE TO ABIDE BY SHOW RULES AND REGULATIONS WHICH APPEAR ON THE REVERSE SIDE OF THIS CONTRACT.

Name of Firm

Address

City   State   Zip

Please indicate below number of booths required.

1. **Southeastern Craft Show - March 12 - 15, 1983**

    Reserve _____ booths

Please refer to attached sheet for rates and description of booth package.

2. We agree to send the full amount for booth space upon acceptance of application. We understand if balance is not paid six (6) weeks prior to the opening of the show, our agreement will be cancelled without refund, and show space will be assigned to another firm.

Signature:

Title:

Please address further exhibit correspondence and bulletins to:
(PLEASE TYPE OR PRINT)

Name and Title

Company

Address

City, State and Zip

Telephone
                        Please include area code and extension

THIS APPLICATION FOR EXHIBIT SPACE IN THE ATLANTA MARKET CENTER IS HEREBY ACCEPTED BY THE ATLANTA MARKET CENTER ON THIS THE _____ DAY OF _____ 19____ .

By:

Title: Craft Show Manager

BASIC TERMS AND CONDITIONS

1. CONTRACT

The application, properly executed by applicant (exhibitor) shall upon written acceptance and notification of booths assigned by Atlanta Market Center constitute a valid and binding contract.

2. ASSIGNMENT OF SPACE

The Atlanta Market Center's assignment of booths is final and shall constitute an acceptance of the exhibitor's offer to occupy space. After assignment, space location may not be changed, transferred or cancelled except upon written request and with the subsequent written approval of the Atlanta Market Center.

Space assignments may be revoked or changed by the Atlanta Market Center at any time that the minimum payment schedule is not met.

3. SUBLETTING

Subletting or licensing of space by the exhibitor or use of the space not authorized by the Atlanta Market Center is prohibited. No exhibitor shall exhibit or permit to be exhibited in the space allotted to him any merchandise other than that specified in the application.

4. EXHIBIT REQUIREMENTS

All booth arrangements shall conform in all respects to the dimensional and height requirements as specified by show management. Exhibitors may not erect or maintain a backwall higher than 8'. No booth may obstruct the general view or access to surrounding displays, aisles or public space within the exhibit facilities. Exhibits must remain in tact until the scheduled hour of conclusion of the show, as such time is established by show management.

5. PAYMENT REQUIREMENTS AND CANCELLATION POLICIES

A 50% minimum deposit (non-refundable) is required with this application. The balance is due no later than 6 weeks prior to the show. Make all checks payable to the Atlanta Market Center, 240 Peachtree Street, Suite 2200, Atlanta, Georgia 30043.

In the event of a cancellation by an exhibitor, it is understood that the Atlanta Market Center reserves the right to reassign cancelled booths without any obligations or refunds to the exhibitor. Exhibit space not claimed by 10:00 a.m. on the opening day of the show reverts back to the Atlanta Market Center to be utilized at the discretion of show management.

Exhibitors shall observe and abide by additional rules or regulations that may be adopted by the Atlanta Market Center which shall be as much as part hereof as though fully incorporated herein. The Atlanta Market Center reserves the right to move or remove an exhibit for the good and welfare of the show.

If the show or any part thereof is prevented from being held, is cancelled by the Atlanta Market Center or the exhibit space applied for therein becomes unavailable because of war, fire, strike, government regulation, public catastrophe, act of God or the public enemy or other cause, the Atlanta Market Center shall determine and refund to the applicant his proportionate share of the balance of the aggregate exhibit fee received which remain after deducting expenses incurred by the Atlanta Market Center and reasonable compensation to the Atlanta Market Center, but in no case shall the amount of refund to the applicant exceed the amount of the exhibit fee paid.

Neither the Atlanta Market Center nor any of their officers, agents, employees and other representatives shall be held accountable or liable for, and the same are hereby released from accountability or liability for, any damage, loss, harm or injury to the person of any property of the applicant or any of its officers, agents, employees or other representatives, resulting from theft, fire, water, accident or any other cause.

The applicant hereby agrees to indemnify, defend and protect the Atlanta Market Center against, and hold harmless from, any and all claims, demand, suits, liability, damages, loss, costs, attorney fees, and expenses or whatever kind of nature which might form or arise out of any action or failure to act of the applicant or any of its officers, agents, employees, or other representatives.

6. LIABILITIES

No demonstrations or solicitations shall be permitted outside of the exhibitors assigned space, and no signs or placards may be displayed on persons or otherwise outside exhibit space. Distribution by the exhibitors of any printed matter, samples or other articles shall be restricted to within the confines of the exhibitor's booth. Exhibitors shall not have or operate any display or exhibit, which, in the sole discretion of the Atlanta Market Center, is the source of objectionable noises or odors or has decorations or other aspects which are considered by the Atlanta Market Center objectionable, including signs, lights, and the costuming of exhibit personnel.

7. DIRECTORY

The Atlanta Market Center will list exhibitor's firm name and space assignment in the official directory. Additional information pertaining to exhibitor's merchandise may be included at the sole discretion of the Atlanta Market Center. However, the Atlanta Market Center will not be responsible for errors or omissions occurring in the printed directory, or for unintentional failure to include an exhibiting firm in the printed directory. It is understood that there will be no samples sales permitted until the last day of the show.

8. COMPLIANCE

The exhibitor assumes all responsibility for compliance with all pertinent ordinances, regulations and codes of duly authorized local, state and federal governing bodies concerning fire, safety and health, together with the rules and regulations of the operators and/or owners of the property wherein the show is held.

9. UNIONS

It is further agreed that the exhibitor will abide by and comply with rules and regulations concerning local unions having agreements with the Atlanta Market Center or with authorized contractors employed by the Atlanta Market Center.

S. E. CRAFTS '83

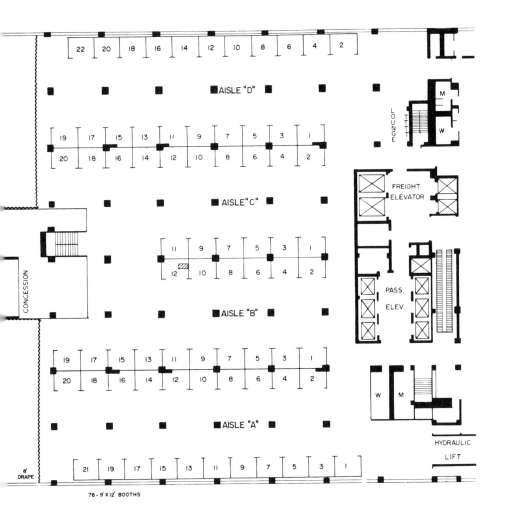

ATLANTA MERCHANDISE MART

□   MARKETING STRATEGIES

Four types of buyers will approach your booth. It will help if you know something of the different markets they are buying for. You are likely to talk to the:

1. Individual Buyer
2. Corporate Buyer
3. Group/Association Buyer
4. Independent Buyer

The Individual Buyer

Representing himself, this buyer usually owns a gallery or two or a small chain of stores and is at the fair to personally select the items that he feels will sell well in his outlets.

The Corporate Buyer

With greater purchasing power, the corporate buyer represents a corporation, like Macy's and is assigned as their buyer in a particular goods line; glasswear, gifts, clothing, etc. The purchase she makes in her specialty area is then distributed throughout the corporation's chain of stores. Obviously the orders can be quite large.

The Group/Association Buyer

This person represents a group of companies that have formed an association to represent them in buying merchandise. Federal regulations prevent the Group/Association buyer from ordering for the associated companies but the buyer recommends purchases. The associated companies pay a great deal of attention to what their buyers say.

The Independent Buyer

This type is a member of an independent buying company which acts as consultants to retail clients. They send out new releases and product updates to inform established clients and others they think will be interested about the latest, hottest products on the market.

The buyers you encounter will be interested in knowing that you are a professional and can deliver. It helps to have order blanks, business cards, a list of wholesale accounts and a DUNS number. A DUNS number is available from Dunn and Bradstreet and provides a sense of stability. The number does not guarantee a good credit rating but does make business transactions easier by putting you in a nationwide computerized business transaction system.

Make sure that you stay in touch with the buyers you have dealt with over the years. If you're just getting started, plan on making a list and keeping it up to date. Why? Let me tell you a story. One year two jewelers were rejected by a wholesale crafts fair, which they had been attending for some years. During the years they had built up a reputation and a following. So when they received a notice of rejection, their initial reaction was one of panic. But level heads won out! The couple rented a hotel room near the fair, and sent notices to all their previous customers to come by for coffee, wine and cheese and see their new line of wares. The results? Excellent!

□ PROMOTING YOURSELF

Unless you have discovered a fantastic new secret to selling, everyone who comes to your booth is not going to buy. But you can do a lot to help future sales by having information available for future buyers. You should make up buyer's packets and give them to every buyer who comes to your booth. Remember that these people are serious buyers with tremendous purchasing power so a little money spent on advertising can reap excellent dividends. It should be designed as a single package including:

1. A resume listing your current wholesale accounts, educational background and other appropriate experiences.
2. A business card.
3. Printed photographs of your work.
4. A catalog. (If you don't have one you should not be in the market).
5. A current price list, including terms and shipping procedures.
6. Any other material that will help to sell your product.

Keep in mind that you have to do a balancing act between the cost of producing your package and the results it produces. The principal reason for the packet is to give the buyer an opportunity to study your work, check with a supervisor and place a sample order. After that your work either sells or it doesn't, but you'll never know until it gets into the stores. Your packet should be attractive, low cost (the lower the cost the more you can pass out) and should provide all the information a buyer needs to order, including an order blank. If this is new to you it will help to get some buyer reaction to your materials and then refine the packet so that it suits their needs. Remember, they are the ones that are doing the purchasing.

□ ANTICIPATE THE SALE

I want to tell you a little story to illustrate an important concept that could mean additional sales to you. Not too long ago I attended a wholesale show for both the giftware market and the craft market. The shows were separate but housed on the same floor so it was easy for the giftware buyers to attend both shows . . . and that was what the show promoters intended. Well, I played the role of a wholesale buyer and attended both shows. To be quite honest I was much more impressed with the quality of the work at the craft show but noticed something about the giftware sellers that I didn't see among the craft sellers.

The giftware sellers assumed that you were going to buy and treated you as a buyer. When I walked up to a booth they greeted me warmly, described what they had on display, handed me descriptive material on their products, told me about shipping dates and made sure that I had their name so that I could contact them personally when I wanted to place my order. At no time did I feel pushed, rather I felt pleased that they gave me so much attention.

Most of the craftsmen I talked to did not anticipate the sale and acted surprised when an order was placed. Attitude is everything! Salesmen are taught to enter into a sales situation believing that the sale has already been made; all they have to do is get the information and work out the details. It's the difference between one Girl Scout knocking on your door and saying "I don't suppose you would want to buy any cookies would you?" and another saying "I'm selling Girl Scout Cookies. Your neighbors are ordering 3 boxes each. Is three boxes going to be enough for you?" One approach anticipates the sale; the other doesn't. What method generates the most sales?

☐ COMPETITION

There is no free lunch and you are not the only person who is serious about making a living in crafts. This means that the top quality wholesale shows are going to attract the top quality craftsmen and you don't get special consideration even if you were an exhibitor last year. You need to apply each year, on an equal basis with other craftsmen. The first hurdle is the juried competition so your presentation should be as professional as possible. Complete the application form completely and legibly and include recent, dated slides of your work. You want everything to work in your favor and I can assure you a jury will react more favorably to an active craftsman (as evidence by you dated work) than one who may not be active.

Every marketing channel has unique features and some crafts-men (because of increased experience) know what works best and what doesn't work. At you first wholesale show make a point to get around to all the other booths to see what's on display and what's going on. Most craftsmen are happy to talk to other craftsmen so don't be afraid to approach them. This is an ideal opportunity to see what the top craftsmen in the country are doing. Check out their displays, their business cards, their order books and anything else you can get access to. If you see an idea you like, try your own version of it at the next show. It just might help your sales.

Remember that the buyers are there to see a wide range of craftsmen and their products, so the people in the booths are sales attractions and are helping your sales. You heard this already in the section on crafts fairs but it is equally true here. Would you pay the booth fee and do all the work of setting up and taking down if you knew that only one buyer would attend the show? Do you think a buyer would fly in all the way from Alaska just to see your crafts?

Make a note of the difference in the crafts in a wholesale show and in a retail show. You will see that some craftsmen completely change their exhibit when the wholesale show is over so they can present a completely different image to the retail buyers. Why? Maybe they know something you don't know. Maybe they have been selling at wholesale shows for years and have a marketing plan all worked out that works for them. Find out if you can.

□ PRICING

We have already reviewed pricing strategies in the introduction to the wholesale marketing channels. However, there are some pricing considerations that are unique to selling at a wholesale crafts fair with which you should be familiar. First, you will be faced with a variety of buyers, ranging from fellow craftsmen who are buying for their own shops to buyers who are placing orders for some of the large department stores.

There will be a tremendous difference in the amount of overhead each buyer has to consider before the product bought from you gets to the retail market. For the fellow craftsman it's simply a matter of doubling the price and putting it on display in his studio. For the volume buyer it means considering the cost of having several different layers of people handle the product before it gets to the showroom.

My suggestion is that you double price all your craft items; the retail and wholesale price. The wholesale price is what you charge any customer, regardless of the size of the order. The retail price suggests to the buyer what it should sell for in her shop. Note that it is only a suggestion because once the product has been purchased from you, you have no control over price.

Double pricing your items may help standardize your prices in the various markets to which they will eventually be retailed. This will help you maintain a standard pricing policy.

□ MARKET CHANNEL SUITABILITY

It is always wise to check something out before you leap into it. Visit one or two wholesale shows and see if you think your work will sell well. Talk to people at the show who have work similar to yours and see how they do.

If you decide to exhibit, remember to estimate the long-term sales effects and not just your actual sales at the show. After you've tried it once, get some perspective on it. When it is time to apply for next year's show, you'll have a good idea if it will be profitable to do it again.

A word of caution: people's tastes change and what sells one year may not sell as well next year. American Craft Enterprises, Inc. publishes a sales summary of each of its fairs so that exhibitors can keep track of trends. One year leather may sell well while the next year sales will drop by 30%. The figures that are the most important are the long term trends, so even if you have a bad show take your overall sales for the year into consideration.

☐ GETTING OUT

Getting out of the wholesale market is easy. Just don't enter any more shows. No slots are held from one year to the next, so if the promoters don't receive you application they won't include you in the show. But, your obligations don't end there. If you have been in previous wholesale shows you have developed accounts with buyers. If they originally met you at a wholesale show they expect to see you there again. If you expect to continue to sell to them you should inform them you are still actively engaged in the crafts business and if they plan to place an order in the future you would like to send them your recent catalog. Inform them that your marketing plans do not include your participation in the wholesale shows.

☐ LEGAL OBLIGATIONS

There are two areas that you need to be knowledgeable about:
1. The contract you sign with the show promoter.
2. The contracts you sign with the buyers at the show.

The show promoter requires that you sign a standard contract, once you have been accepted into the show. The contract will state in clear terms what you are responsible for and what the sponsor is responsible for. Read the contract carefully. If you have any questions ask and if you don't agree with anything don't sign. The signed contract, together with your booth rental fee constitute your acceptance of the terms and your acceptance, by the sponsors as an exhibitor.

Any order you sign with a buyer should be considered a legal contract. Remember that these buyers have tremendous buying power and are taking a chance when they order form you. If you don't come through they look bad and they have the right to sue you for breach of contract. Remember to, that a buyer is representing perhaps hundreds of stores or clients and if he promises them each 100 widgets in time for Christmas and you sign a contract that you will have those widgets for him, both of you are accepting a lot of responsibility. If you don't produce you'll catch hell from the buyer, but she'll catch hell from 100 customers. And you can be sure that that buyer will not order from you again.

Some buyers will simply write an order for what they want and ask if you can fill it by a certain date. If you say yes, they'll say "Ok, you've got a deal. Send it when it's done." This sort of verbal/written document is not legally binding but should be considered as such by the craftsperson. The bottom line in the crafts business is quality and responsibility. If you have a quality product and conduct yourself in a professional, businesslike manner your business will continue to grow. Remember that the secret to success is repeat business and by treating each order as a contract and delivering on time you will gain the respect of your customer and will get the repeat orders that you want and need.

☐ WHOLESALE BUYERS MARKET REVIEW

1. Wholesale shows offer tremendous exposure. Each buyer represents many future outlets.
2. Booth fees can be expensive, ranging from $50 to $500.
3. Check out the reliability of the show's sponsors, particularly if the show is a new one.
4. Check out sales figures from previous years if it is an established show.
5. Buyers feel more comfortable placing orders with craftspeople who have demonstrated that they can handle wholesale accounts.
6. Be honest about your production ability. Don't accept orders that you will be unable to fill.
7. Prepare promotional materials that buyers can take with them. Your promotional package should contain everything a buyers needs to order from you in the future.
8. Use every wholesale show as an educational experience. See what fellow craftspeople are doing.
9. Know what you need to get for your crafts *before* you enter the show and stick to that price. Many wholesale buyers will ask for a discount (2-10% is common). If you cannot offer a discount and still make a profit don't.
10. Always have samples of new items. A wholesale show is a great place test their marketability.
11. A wholesale buyers is interested in your abilities as a businessman first, your abilities as a craftsman second.
12. There is a tremendous mark-up on items because of the number of people involved in getting the product to the customer. The mark-up can reach five times your selling cost.
13. Wholesale buyers deal in volume. Are you ready and/or able to produce in the numbers they request?

Chapter 13

Selling to Department Stores and Other Volume Dealers

Department stores throughout the country are featuring more and more hand-made items. Neiman-Marcus has been selling quality crafts for years and recently J.C. Penney has begun a crafts retailing program in some of its stores. Between these two extremes there are hundreds of store chains that market crafts. You might want to refer to *Department Stores and Mail Order Firms*, available from Business Guides, Inc.; 425 Park Avenue; New York, NY 10022 for a list of department stores that you could contact. If can be very lucrative if you have the right product because a chain store can sell thousands of your items. But you must be able to produce these thousands of items, maintain quality and make a profit. If you can't do all these things, don't be afraid to say no to large volume selling.

Within the last few years, Many department stores have added a mail order component to their marketing program. Catalog departments offers an ideal outlet for craftspeople as their catalogs usually feature unique, expressive, one-of-a-kind items.

Should you decide to sell to department stores, your accounts can range from a small local department store that features crafts in a display at the check-out counter to an account with a nation-wide chain of stores that averages thousands of dollars a month.

□ LOCATING VOLUME BUYERS

Any department store or other volume buyer is a potential customer, but before you go to the large outlets it's best to establish your credibility. I'd recommend that you call on some local stores so that you become familiar with the way department stores do business. Make an advice call on two or three stores to see how they buy their merchandise. Remember that you are not selling to them, you are only getting advice, and some familiarity with selling terms.

Do some research in your area. Tour the department stores to determine which sell crafts. These stores are naturals for an advice call. Contact the giftware buyer (that's usually the person who buys crafts) and ask for her advice. Call the giftware buyer and ask for her name. When the buyer comes to the phone, address her by name and say, "Ms. Freemoney? My name is _____. I'm interested in the possibility of selling my handmade toys to department stores such as yours. I notice that your store does sell handmade crafts and I'm calling to get advice. Could we set up a time at your convenience to get together? I'd like to show you what I make and get your opinion as to whether it might be suitable for department store sales."

The buyer, whether she actually buys from you or not, is going to be very valuable to you. Your objective is to become more familiar with this particular marketing channel so don't be afraid to ask questions such as:

1. Do you think my crafts would sell well?
2. What other stores might be interested?
3. Is my selling price low enough so that the mark-up can be added and still sell at a reasonable price?
4. What could I do to make my presentation or my product more saleable in this market?

Ask the buyer for sample copies of order blanks and contracts they use with their suppliers.

You might ask the buyer where she locates the products she buys. Write down what she says! If she goes to three wholesale shows a year, find out which ones they are. If she order through catalogs, get their names and publishers. If she orders directly from some craftspeople, ask to see their marketing packages. Do this with a small store buyer; they'll have more time (maybe), but usually they are more helpful than big chain buyers.

When you have completed your research it is time to test the market. Remember that it is very competitive and the initial impression you project had better be a good one or you can forget your chances of being considered. You may wish to contact some volume buyers by mail, but I would wait on this until you have a professional-looking presentation that includes a brochure, price list, covering letter, etc.

The best place to begin is by contacting volume buyers personally. Contact people that you know about from your earlier advice calls.

□ MARKET STRATEGIES

The person you talk to who is in a position to buy your crafts is not automatically going to buy. You have to face this from the beginning. It is nothing personal; it is based on your craft work and your ability to honor any contractual agreements you may enter into. Here is a step-by-step guide to making a sale.

1. Look professional! You are in the business world now and need to dress accordingly. A suit, business dress or sport coat and tie are essential. You'll gain ground here immediately because the

buyer will probably not expect you to present such a professional image.

2. Have your samples professionally displayed. If they are small, carry them in an attache case. If it's jewelry, have them mounted on velvet; ceramic pieces can be carefully wrapped in tissue paper or white felt, etc., etc.

3. Do your homework! Know where they are already selling crafts (if they are), know how many stores they have, basic selling terms, contract terms, etc., etc. The more you know about them, the more impressed they will be with you!

4. Leave an illustrated catalog and price list with her. They may want a day or so to decide or they may need to check with the head buyer. Have some material that they can use to refresh their memory or refer to the head buyer.

5. Leave a business card. Many buyers will keep these for a long time and the buying patterns of stores do change. You just may get a call in six or nine months.

6. Leave a list of references and of galleries and shops you sell to. Even if your crafts are super, they're going to be leery because craftspeople have a reputation for being independent free spirits. After all, don't craftspeople make crafts because they can't make it in the business world? If you've made sales to other department stores, this is the time to share that information. Anything you can do to project the image of a solid reliable, responsible businessperson is only going to help you.

7. Some department stores have buyers days. This can be very discouraging and you may feel it is beneath you. Here's how it works! One day a week is scheduled as buyers day. Anyone wishing to show their products to the department store buyers must schedule a time for that particular day. Usually the time allocated is short, 15 to 30 minutes. You may feel like you are a number being herded through, but you just may get a sale. It's up to you to decide whether you want to go through this process or not.

□   HOW TO PROMOTE YOUR WORK

Similar techniques of promotion are used regardless of the marketing channel you are currently employing. By all means, use all the traditional techniques of demonstrations, information flyers, news releases, television and radio spots, and anything else you can think of. Just be sure to clear everything with the department store or other volume buyer you sell to.

The promotional concept you want to develop most thoroughly after you sell the first department store is developing sales to other department stores. Remember you are plowing new ground here. Once you have a track record with one store, you should let other stores know that the arrangement has worked out successfully for you and the department store. You are, in a sense, telling them that you have experience, that you've proved yourself.

Take photos of your display in the store, summarize the sales that you had and, if you can, get something in writing from the buyer. Tell her that naturally you will offer her store an exclusive in this area, but you do have the capacity to expand. Would she mind making a few comments (in writing) about your business conduct and the quality of your work. Not every buyer responds, but if you can get one or two to do so, you're in!! Try it.

The department store buyer will keep you informed on the sales of your work. Nobody can tell ahead of time what will sell and what won't. You'll probably sell a sample order and then replace what sells. I think the important thing here is to go out of your way to make sure that you respond to what the department store or other volume buyer wants. When you've proved yourself then you can contact other volume outlets.

□   COMPETITION

When you sell to department stores, you'll find that there is very little competition from other craftsmen. The main competitive threat will come from the manufactured items on display near your work. The secret to overcoming the competition is to make your crafts so unique that there is nothing like it in the store.

The department store buyer will be looking for two things when considering purchase of your work:

1. Will your crafts sell in a department store?
2. Can you produce in volume and keep the orders filled?

If the answer is yes to both of those questions and continues to be yes, you should have little or no competition. Be assured that the department store will feature the work of other craftsmen if they find that yours sells well, but as long as you can keep them supplied they probably will not handle any other crafts that directly compete with yours. However, should your work stop selling, or should you be unable to keep them supplied, they will look elsewhere.

□   PRICING

Pricing is crucial! You must know from the start the price you must receive to make a profit. If you can't get your price don't sell, period. If you had a couple of hours to spare, I could tell you all kinds of horror stories about craftsmen getting caught in a volume-price-sales trap.

Volume buyers expect to pay a lower price for your work than others. They'll carefully point out that their overhead and sales costs are higher, so in order to price your product competitively, they'll need to buy at a lower price. Notice that they are not proposing that they make any sacrifice, but want you to.

How do you deal with the pressure to lower your price? Tell

the buyer, "I know that you have carefully calculated your mark-up so that you can expect to make a reasonable profit. I have done the same thing. My price list reflects what I need to charge for each of my pieces. Unlike other products that can be mass produced at a lower per-item cost, each one of my products is hand made and takes the same time to produce whether I make one or one thousand. Let me suggest a compromise. Why don't you try a sample order in one of your stores. Add whatever mark-up you need and see if my work sells. If it does, I can supply you with more, if it doesn't neither of us has suffered."

□   MARKET SUITABILITY

You do not *have* to sell in any market channel that is unprofitable to you. That sound obvious but there are craftsmen who lost their objectivity when offered a contract by Neiman-Marcus or Saks Fifth Avenue.

I say again, know up front what you need to get for each one of your crafts items in order to make a profit. If you can't get your price, don't sell! Before you decide that volume selling is unprofitable for you, look at all your expenses and your work habits. If there is a small difference in the price you are offered and the price you need to get, you may be able to make your operation more efficient and lower your per item price!

□   LEGAL RESPONSIBILITIES

You should expect to sign a contract with the department store when you make a sale. They will come in all sizes and description, but they all contain three ingredients: the offer, the acceptance, and the consideration.

Let's say you make wooden toys. You meet with the buyer of the department store, show her your toys and suggest that she buy them (that's the offer). The buyer says she will buy because she thinks they will sell (the acceptance). Both of you then agree on what the price will be (the consideration). Naturally, you agree to put this all down in writing. You, as the craftsperson, agree to deliver twelve wooden cars, six wooden trains and ten airplanes priced respectively at $6.95, 19.95 and 12.95 each. You further agree to deliver them on or before June 1st, with the bill to be paid within 60 days of invoice date.

Under the contract described above, you are legally bound to deliver the goods as described on the specified date and the store is obligated to pay the agreed-up price within sixty days. What happens if you don't deliver? There is some interpretation of the law required here. If you deliver two weeks late, under normal circumstances, the store is still liable for payment. However, if the store had planned to use your toys as part of their main Christmas display "Babes in Toyland," and you were two weeks late, the store could justifiably refuse to accept your order.

Be sure to get all your contracts in writing because, being a conscientious craftsperson, you will honor your part of the contract, so a written contract is just protection for you.

□   GETTING OUT

If you've taken the time at the beginning to make sure you can make money on a volume basis, then chances are slim that you will need or want to get out. If you do need to get out, there is little problem in doing so. When you contract with a department store to fill an order, you must deliver. Once they accept the order and pay you for it, the contract is legally ended. However, you should keep in touch, and, by all means, let them know that you don't intend or aren't able to fill future orders. They will have to make alternative plans and want to know ahead of time. You're not required to tell them of your intentions, but it sure helps with public relations. And, of course, the only reason you will be getting out of volume selling is that you have developed another market(s) more profitable for you.

□   DEPARTMENT STORES AND OTHER VOLUME MARKETS REVIEW

1. This marketing channel is developing rapidly..
2. Be realistic about your production capabilities.
3. Start small with local department stores.
4. One or two reliable volume accounts can help your cash flow.
5. Do not commit more than 20% of your total sales to volume markets. Otherwise, if one closes, you'll be in a bind!
6. Be prepared for a 60 day or longer payment period.
7. Don't commit yourself to high volume production and its potential problems until you are sure you can handle it.
8. Experience counts! Show that you can handle accounts with small clients and larger orders will be forthcoming.
9. Know what you must charge for each product to make a profit and never sell for less.
10. When entering the market make some advice calls to learn market procedures and terms.
11. Present yourself professionally at all times.
12. Have professional-looking materials to leave with the buyer.
13. Be prepared to sign and honor contracts.

PART FOUR

Other Profitable
Marketing Channels

Chapter 14

Overview of Other Marketing Strategies

Some market channels are so unique that they need to be treated individually and marketing strategies need to be developed to suit each particular channel. Unusual marketing channels each have their pitfalls and rewards.

☐ ADVANTAGES

The real advantage of selling crafts in non-traditional markets is that you often have the market almost exclusively to yourself. At the very least you are faced with far less competition than in traditional markets. Some of the market channels we'll be talking about in this section, commission sales and mail order, are really not all that unusual from a marketing standpoint but there are special considerations that can make the difference between success and failure.

☐ DISADVANTAGES

Selling crafts in non-traditional markets presents a higher risk factor. Most craftsmen sell successfully in the wholesale and retail markets. They may make some mistakes and often don't make as much profit as they would like, but sales are fairly consistent. Trying a new market is not as rewarding because you are trying to attract an audience that may not be familiar with crafts and some of the successful marketing strategies may not be as well known to you.

☐ DEVELOPING A STRATEGY

As you will see when you read about other marketing channels it is essential that you develop strategies that work for you. Commission selling, for example, is a very personal business and you will need to make contacts with individuals who are in a position to buy or know people who have buying and decision making power. In mail order you'll see that what your product is really makes little difference because anything you can think of has been successfully sold by mail — including ant farms, real estate, medicine, movies, franchises, artificial limbs, stocks, bonds, time-share vacation homes, university degrees, tax shelters and much much more. What does matter is how you present your product. You've got to know how to promote your product to a specific audience in a particular advertising media.

If you are interested in selling to markets which I have grouped under "unusual craft outlets" you'll need to stay in touch with those markets to see who needs what, at what price and at what time.

A final word. High risk investments tend to return the greatest yield. Unusual craft markets could very well return the highest sales and profits.

Chapter 15

Commissions

A commission is essentially an agreement to execute an idea. Most often the client has an idea, asks the craftspeople to execute the project but does not know exactly what it will look like or what the effect will be until the work is completed. It's important that the client and the craftspeople stay in touch from the beginning to the end and it's important that the commission be completed in stages with both parties agreeing to each stage before the next one is completed.

□ WHAT TO EXPECT

Although craftspeople are doing more commissions, the percentage of craftspeople doing commissions remains small. If you're new to commission work, there are some things you need to be aware of before you get started. Commissions can be rewarding but you can get burned too! It's essential that you know what is expected of you and that you know you can honor your part of the contract.

Advantages
Commissions are exciting. They give you a chance to exercise your creative abilities to their fullest. Very often they give you a chance to try a new process, develop a new idea or refine an old one. Simply working on a larger scale than in production work is also rewarding. Everything changes when you work ten to one hundred times your regular scale; color relationships, textures, values, shapes, etc.

Commissions are more rewarding financially. Because you are executing a one-of-a-kind piece designed for a specific client, you should expect to be rewarded more highly for your efforts than for production work. Naturally, as your experience and reputation grows, you'll be able to demand (and get) more for your services.

Commissions create other commissions, so it's a great way to promote yourself. Architects, interior designers, and art consultants are always looking for new ideas and new artists. The fact that you have successfully completed one or more commissions indicates that you are a professional artist/craftsman who can deal with this aspect of the business world.

Every commission gives you an opportunity to shape the aesthetic sensibility of the public. Most commissions are not done for museums, but for public places, i.e., auditoriums, parks, hotels, office buildings, airports, etc. Several large works were commissioned for the new Harsfield International Airport in Atlanta, Georgia. The works created quite a controversy, but they are seen by literally millions of people each year.

Disadvantages

Some craftspeople have been hurt financially on commissions because they didn't handle the business side correctly. There are specific steps that need to be taken in the contracting of any commission. If you are just getting started, it's easy to get so excited that you agree to do a piece for a certain amount of money, shake hands, and head for the studio to start working. When the piece is done (after hundreds or thousands of hours of work) the client refuses it saying "That's not what we had agreed upon at all."

It's also possible to lose money because of faulty accounting procedures. It's difficult to know how to estimate all the costs until you have done a few commissions, so sometimes items are left out when producing the estimate. You may find yourself barely breaking even or losing money on your first commission, but it probably won't happen again because you'll remember to include the cost of airfare to and from the installation site, installation preparation and hanging and all the "little things" that add up.

Sometimes craftsmen get themselves in real difficulty when they force the materials to do what they were not intended for. A clay that works well for mugs and casseroles will probably not be suitable for a 12 x 24 foot ceramic architectural commission. Are you really sure that the 100% wool yarn that you have been using for years for your placemats is what you want to use in the tapestry you've been commissioned to do for the public library?

Experience is extremely helpful in commission work because you learn what materials work for you. But beware at the beginning and test everything so that you can deliver what you promise. Any necessary research and testing should be included in your initial proposal although you should not call it that because it may give the impression that you don't know what you are doing. Include your essential testing under the category of design or site analysis.

□ COMPETITION

You should know right up front that other craftsmen will be competing for the same commissions. That really shouldn't bother you — after all, you were not prevented from becoming a craftsman just because there already were some other craftsmen. Present yourself in a professional manner, demonstrate what you can do and you'll get commissions.

You will be working primarily with architects, interior designers and art consultants so it is your job to show them what you can do. If you are well prepared you will win more than your share of commissions. Don't expect to win every one, but keep in mind that exposure is good for you.

You can significantly increase your success rate by doing one thing better than your competitors; being more professional. Your portfolio is obviously important, but the client is primarily interested in one thing; "Will it work?" If you have an established track record and can cite statistics and examples from previous commissions it will help tremendously. Suppose a client is impressed with your proposal but wants to know how the commission will be installed. You could say:

"An installation this size requires certain preparations that many weavers are not familiar with. First the entire piece is reinforced with a noninflammatory fabric that is bonded to the weaving with a permanent latex material. This backing is not seen from the front and allows the fabric to hang naturally but prevents it from stretching. Because of the weight of the fabric it will be mounted to the wall in twelve different locations. . . ."

Compare that explanation with this one:

"Oh! I've never done anything this large before but it really is the same thing as my small pieces. I'll just use more glue to stick it to the wall. . . ."

Which presentation would you be the most impressed with? The message is, the more professional your presentation the more commissions you are going to be awarded.

□ ENTERING THE MARKET

Because most commissions come through interior designers, architects and art consultants, this is where you need to begin your research. Before approaching them you will want to understand their professions and in the course of doing so make some advice calls. Obviously if you've already done commissions, you have established contacts that you will want to maintain but you should be continually developing new ones.

There are some excellent publications that will give you an idea of what is currently happening and will suggest areas that you will want to explore. Some of the magazines dealing with architectural commissions are *Interior Design, DOMUS, Progressive Architecture*, and *Arts and Architecture*. There are newsletters and other publications available in any field that you are interested in. You might try *The Encyclopedia of Associations* as well. Interior designers, architects and art consultants all belong to professional organizations. The magazines and newsletters published by these organizations can be tremendously helpful in searching out possible sources of new commissions. They are all listed in the *Encyclopedia of Associations*.

Now's the time to put on your Sherlock Holmes hat because you will be out searching for clues. Let's say that you discover an article on a mural that was done for the East Peoria Library. In reading the article you note that a Mr. Ralph Klondike headed up the selection committee, that the money for the project was donated by the Ladies Aid Society and that the work was done by a mosaic craftsman named Sidney Blum. All three sources will provide valuable information for you. Write, or better still, call them and ask your questions.

Use your time effectively by researching the areas you want to work in. If you design fabrics you need to establish contacts in the fabric manufacturing business, if you want to work through interior designers obviously you need to get in touch with some interior designers. At this stage you are searching for more information and are not looking for specific commissions. When I was researching this chapter I contacted two interior designers to learn how successful craftsmen contacted interior designers to show their work. Those two sources alone gave me enough information to write a book on the interior designer/craftsperson business arrangement. They knew who the head of every interior design firm was, what they were and were not looking for, and who to contact in each firm to show your work.

The message I got from all the people I contacted was, "This is a very personal business and it really helps to have contact and use them." You get contacts, as if you didn't already know, from advice calls. And by all means keep track of who said what, when and where.

Let's assume that you have done your research and have come to the conclusion that there is a market for your woven tapestries. The next thing is to set up appointments with people who are in positions to buy your work and show them what you do.

You can take one of two approaches to set up your appointments. If you don't know the firm or the person in charge you need to take the:

Cold Approach
Write to the firms you are interested in, tell them why you are writing, give a brief overview of your background and experience and ask for an appointment to talk with them. Do not send your vita and other supportive materials at this time. Your objective is to create enough interest that they will want to talk to get the rest of the story about you and your work.

If you're going to make it in this business you're going to need a professional image and presentation. Your stationery represents you and is the first thing the prospective client sees so it had better make a favorable impression. Do not write on personal stationery! You are contacting this person because you hope to do business with his company, not take him sailing on your boat or invite him to your daughter's wedding.

Address your letter to the president of the company! If you don't know the president's name there is handy reference manual called *Contact Influential*. It lists the names of all the company presidents by state and zip code. Check with your local library or send for your own copy. The address is *Contacts Influential*, Weather Bldg, 10th Floor, 516 S.E. Morrison, Portland, Oregon (503) 236-2141.

Don't take it personally, but you'll get very few replies from your letters so you'll need to follow up with a phone call in about ten days. When the person you wrote comes to the phone, say, "Ms. Pettibone? My name is Wanda Weaver. I sent you a letter a few days ago outlining my background and experience in architectural scale weavings. I am going to be in your area Monday and Tuesday of next week and am calling to set up an appointment at a time that would be convenient for you. Is Monday or Tuesday better?"

Note what occurred during the conversation. First, you didn't criticize her for not responding to your letter and second, you gave her a choice between two dates. Don't let her choose any time because she very well may say, "I'm tied up all this week. Call again in two or three weeks."

Don't let any opportunity go untried. If you are turned down or put off until another time use the present contact on the phone to thank them for their time and consideration. If you have been turned down outright (it happens to all of us) send a letter in a day or so, include your promotional materials and a cover letter stating your understanding of their present decision not to consider your work and expressing your hope that they will keep your materials on file for possible future consideration. If you are asked to call back in a week or so, make sure that you do and remind the company president that it was he/she who asked you to call back.

When you do show up for your appointment the first thing your prospective client is going to see is you. Keep in mind that stereotypes persist, so some of the clients you meet are going to fully expect you to arrive in paint-stained coveralls with a beret on your head. Favorable initial impressions are essential and dramatically improve your chances for success. Dress like a professional! Because this is a busness call the more you dress like your prospective client the better off you'll be. Why? Because you want her to feel that you are a member of the team.

Allow me to relate a little story that reinforces my point. Each profession has its uniform. When I first started calling on businesses I wore my college professor uniform and was disappointed with the reception that I received. Everyone was cordial but there was a barrier between us that was impossible to get over. A discussion of the situation with an old and honest friend identified the problem. I didn't look the part of a businessman, therefore, I couldn't know anything about the business world. Because of my uniform I was perceived as a visitor or even worse, an intruder.

The transformation began after some initial research into the businessman's domain. I treated myself to a series of business lunches and simply observed what businessmen wore. In a very short time I had identified three different uniforms and promptly went out and bought two complete outfits. The outfits are worn anytime I want to talk with anyone in the business community. It cost me money but it has made far more money for me than the initial cost. I consider it one of my best investments!

The second most important selling tool is your portfolio. Naturally it will include photographs of your work, a list of commissions you have done and a brief summary of your educational experience and

4/82

BIOGRAPHICAL INFORMATION

Margaret Groff Agner
320 Snapfinger Dr.
Athens, Georgia 30605
Phone (404) 353-7719

Birthplace: Continental, Ohio 3/20/43

Academic Career: Liberal Arts and art studies at Antioch College, 1961-63. Rochester Institute of Technology, School of Art & Design, Rochester, N.Y. 1963-64. BFA in painti from LSU, 1974; additional Literature courses. Numero painting, design, and dye and fiber workshops and seminars.

Professional Career: Painting since 1965--acrylic, w/c, pastel, oil. Silk screen printing, 1968-73. Batik since 1973. Design an construction of large liturgical banners, altar and pulpit pieces etc. since 1972 (17 pieces owned by University United Methodist Church, Baton Rouge). Teaching children's and adults' classes in art since 1974. Teaching 3-day workshops in batik since 1977. Judging art shows, Louisiana, 1975-79.

Commissions: Exxon, stitchery wall hangings, 6/78. Lobby of office building, Scenic Highway, Baton Rouge. Many private commissions.

Awards: 2nd place in painting, Summer Festival 1977, Baton Rouge. Semi-finalist, Public Walls program, Baton Rouge, 1977. Louisiana Crafts Council Juried Stitcher Show, Honorable Mention 11/78. 1st place drawing, Acadian Art Festival, 10/78. 1st place for batik boot Louisiana Art and Artists' Guild Octoberfest, 1978. Painting purchased by Centroplex (City Hall), Baton Rouge. Merit award for silk painting process, Albany Arts Festival, 4/82.

Exhibitions, Juried Shows: Louisiana State Professional Exhibitions, 1974-76. F Smith, Ark. 25th and 27th Annual Competition. Louisiana Crafts Council, Louisiana Craftsmen's Show 1975, 76, 78, 79. Barnwell Center, Shreveport, La., Annual Juried Show, 1976. Ohio Drawing and Print Sho 1971. Print Club of Albany (N.Y.) 1971. Arkansas Art Center, 10th Annual Prints, Drawings and Crafts professional training. You should have extra copies of your vita and photos to leave with your client.

Here are two examples that fabric designer Margaret Agner uses to promote her work. You will want to approach your promotional material in your own way but you should have them and they should look professional.

Margaret G. Agner / page 2

Exhibition, 1977. LSU Union, 5 Contemporary Galleries Show, 6/77. River Road Show National Juried Exhibition, Baton Rouge, 5/78, 5/79. St. Tammany Art Association Delta Primate Center Show, 7/78. Baton Rouge Gallery Christmas Shows, 1977, 79. Louisiana Watercolor Society National Exhibition, 1977, 78. Spectrum Show, Lyndon House Art Center, Athens, Ga. 11/79, 11/80. Georgia Designer Craftsmen Juried Traveling Show, 1979-80, Savannah, Columbus, Madison and Albany, Ga. Second Biennial 4-State Thread & Fiber Competition, Alexandria Museum, Alexandria, La. 1979. Southeast '80 Craft Competition, LeMoyne Art Foundation, Tallahassee, Fla., 5/80. Atlanta Arts Festival, Artists' Market, 5/80, 5/81, 5/82. Contemporary Crafts of Northeast Georgia, Quinlan Art Center, Gainesville, Ga. 10/80. Baltimore Winter Market of American Crafts, 2/81. Thread & Fiber - A Common Ground, Alexandria, La. Museum Juried Biennial Exhibition, 9/81. 10th Annual Ringling Museums Crafts Festival, Sarasota, Fla. 11/81. Elegance II, national invitational, Westlake Gallery, White Plains, N.Y. 3/82. National Contemporary American Crafts: Pottery, Glass, Metal, Wood and Fiber: Arts Signature, Tulsa, Okla. 11/81.

e or
o-man Shows: Baton Rouge Little Theater, 1/77, Baton Rouge, La., one-man. Zigler Museum, Jennings, La. 2/79, all fiber show, one-man. University United Methodist Church, 4/79, Baton Rouge, La., one-man. Savannah College of Art & Design, Savannah, Ga. 8/80, with Susan Loftin. A Touch of Glass Gallery, Decatur, Ga. 7/81, with Gordon Batten. The Art Gallery in Athens, Athens, Ga. one-man, 9/81. Rizzoli Gallery, Atlanta, Ga. (the Omni) 10/81, with Susan Thomas. Women's Commission Gallery, Defiance College, Defiance, Ohio 2/82, one-man.

:
ganizations: Spectrum, Inc., Athens, Ga., Juried member, board member. Athens Fibercraft Guild, Athens, Ga., board member. Georgia Mountain Crafts. Surface Design Association.

Margaret Agner
320 Snapfinger Drive
Athens, Georgia 30605
(404) 353-7719

8 *Quadricentric Dance*
40" × 40"   Edition 18

7 *Winged Choreographer*
40" × 72" or 111" Edition 12

28 *Unicorns Drinking*
40" × 73"   Edition 15

2 *The Enchanted Land*
40" × 77"   Ed

9 *The Bath*
26" × 37"   Edition 24

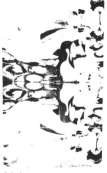
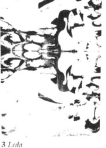

3 *Leda*
40" × 72"   Edition 15

4 *Arcadia*
40" × 65"   Edition 15

23 *Resurrection*
40" × 51" or 74"   Edit

15 *Virgin & Unicorn*
19" × 26" Edition 24

13 *Pegasus at Night*
19" × 31"
Edition 24

11 *Pegasus with Horse*
19" × 45" Edition 24

10 *Autumn Scene*
19" × 45" Edition 24

12 *Standing Virgin
& Unicorn*
19" × 45" Edit

24 *Flock of Sheep*
14"   Edition 30

17 *Mermaid Combing
Her Hair*
19" × 31" Edition 24

27 *Unicorn Head*
10"

Edition 40

25 *Fish*
14"
Edition 30

Don't be surprised if, when you arrive for the appointment, the receptionist says "Oh yes Ms. Weaver! Ms. Pettibone is in a critical meeting. You'll be meeting with Mr. Bumbles" (Mr. Bumbles is the youngest and least experienced member of the firm). It happens all the time and is not to be taken personally. The trick is to so impress Mr. Bumbles that he will call in a superior or two and you can then talk to someone in a position of authority.

Not every appointment is going to lead to a commission offer immediately. That's why it's important to have materials you can leave for them to look at later, share with their colleagues and keep on file for future use. And by all means, keep in touch by sending updates of your recent work.

The Warm Approach

You will quickly see how much better this approach is. Most craftspeople use this approach whenever possible, but still use the cold approach from time to time. The warm approach is based on *personal* contact.

First, you have the name of the person you are going to call because it was given to you by someone you talked to in a previous advice call. Don't send a letter in the warm approach. Call direct! When your prospective client comes to the phone say "Mr. Hardwall? My name is Wesley Weaver. I recently completed a commission for Sam Teesquare and he felt that some of the design concepts I used might interest you for your new Government Park Office Complex. I'm going to be in your city Monday and Tuesday of next week for some other appointments and would like to come by and show you my work. Which day is better for you?"

See how nice and easy that was? And chances are that you will be seen right away by the head man, the person who has the power to decide, and that's what you want. The cold or warm approach can be used in any situation whether you are talking to an architect about a weaving for the lobby of the hotel he is designing, or with a carpet designer about doing some free-lance design commissions. The more people you talk to the more commissions you'll get, and remember to get those referrals!

Each contact you develop has done business with at least ten other people who probably will be interested in your product. . .and all of those are warm contacts. Referrals are any salesman's bread and butter and they will be yours too because you are selling your skills and expertise!

□ MARKETING STRATEGIES

In seeking commissions you will have to make three distinct types of presentations. One will be to an agent who will act as a representative for you, i.e., an interior designer, architect or art consultant. The second will be made directly to the client and the third will be made to a commission committee. The approaches you need to take are different in each but there is one rule that applies in every instance: Listen to the client's wants and needs. If a client feels you can fill those wants and needs better than the other applicants, you will get the commission. It's as simple as that. Unfortunately, many craftsmen are so involved in their own thing that they fail to listen to what the client is asking for. Consequently they don't get the commission. My advice is: "Shut up and listen to what the people who sign the checks are telling you." There's plenty of room for negotiation after you get the go ahead to design a model.

Working With an Agent

It is always a worthwhile experience to reverse roles once in a while. If you are selling to galleries put yourself in the gallery owner's position. How would you react to the work produced in your studio? If you were an agent what would you look for in a craftsman you were representing? An agent is your representative and acts as the intermediary between you and the client. As such, an agent can point out things that a client may feel but be unwilling to tell you directly. As an example, a client may like your work but be unconvinced about your reliability. You and your agent can work together to convince the client that you can deliver what you promise.

Usually an agent represents several different craftspeople. It is your job to make sure that your agent clearly understand what is unique about your work. Your first priority in making a presentation to an agent is to convince him that you are a professional and know what you are doing. After all, the agent, if he agrees to represent you, is putting his own reputation on the line because if a client is not satisfied with the final work he will go after the agent, not you. And if you don't perform as stated in the contract neither you nor the agent gets paid.

Anything you can do to develop your professional relationship with the agent is an asset. Provide him with descriptive literature and photos of your work, samples if appropriate, letters of recommendation from previous clients, etc., etc. The agent should also know what your work is all about so that he can effectively represent you. It isn't enough for him to know that you work in wood, he should know that you use the surface texture of wood and wood shapes to reflect the interior light of spaces so that as the day changes your forms pick up and play on that light. . . . or whatever it is that you do. And by all means provide examples of how you have successfully executed your concepts.

Don't forget to involve the agent in the process as much as possible. Everyone likes to feel that they are in charge, so let the agent feel that he or she has played a major role in getting you and the client together (it's probably true anyway). Remember, the more the agent feels part of the process the better he or she will represent you.

Approaching the Client Directly

This is a little bit different situation because there is no middleman and consequently no buffer between artist and client. It is your responsibility to find out what the client wants and to determine whether you want to or can fill those wants.

Remember that your client's first priority is to fill his wants, not yours. Suppose, for example, that the client is a restaurant owner and wants a wall mural. Find out why! Listen to what he wants because this is where you begin your negotiation. If he simply wants to decorate a wall he could use wallpaper or paint; there must be another reason. In almost every instance the client has a *single* most important reason for wanting a commission piece. If you can discover this reason you are halfway to a signed contract.

When you have determined why the client wants a particular commission executed, you can begin your educational process. If the client wants a wall hanging to reduce noise in a room you can explain how your design will do just that. As a good craftsman you must find a way to make an aesthetically sound design within these constraints.

In almost every instance the client has an idea of what he or she wants. That simple idea gives you plenty of time to exercise your creative abilities, but there is one point that cannot be emphasized enough: *When you do commissions you must assure the client that you are translating his or her wishes into a work of art.* People engage an architect because they want to design "their house." In executing commissions you are performing in a similar role in that you are assisting your client in putting his ideas into tangible form.

Corporate and Government Commissions

It's difficult enough translating your client's wishes into an art form. What do you do if the client doesn't know what he wants? This is often the case with corporate and government commissions, particularly when the committee's charge is selection of an artist. You may deal with a corporate or government client directly or through an agent but the problems are just the same — bureaucracy. Nobody, it seems, wants to take the responsibility of making a decision. When forced to decide, they avoid the issue by exclaiming "You know I believe that is really something our architectural department should decide upon. Give Fred Johnson a call and see what he has to say. If he approves it I'll certainly go along with it."

Governmental commissions are even more difficult to deal with because of the additional red tape involved and the fact that they are almost always administered by committees, not at just one level but at several different levels. By the time the original idea goes through all the government branches and each administrator makes a modification (to justify his existence?) the original idea has little resemblance to the final form.

My advice? Hang in there! Once you are involved in the process you can usually find one member of the committee who can give you straight answers to your questions and can help things proceed almost normally. The often repeated quote "When in Rome. . ." is appropriate here.

□ PRICING

Careful planning will ensure that a commission will be profitable for you. Harden yourself to the idea that your clients will always think your prices too high. That's because commissions of art work is usually a new field for them and there are no pre-established guidelines for them to follow. In the construction industry, building and labor costs are fairly standard so there are guidelines to compare one company's bid with another. But how do you put a price on art? Do you charge by the square foot, or charge for materials plus labor or what?

It is your responsibility to educate your client. After all, you are the expert and nobody knows better than you what is involved in the project. Be professional and present your proposal and its cost with no apologies. Your presentation should include a description of how you arrived at your contract figures and how much you are charging for materials, labor, installation and overhead. If the client accepts your proposal, you can proceed with the assurance that you will profit from the experience. If the proposal is refused you have lost a minimum amount of time and effort and can begin preparing for another.

□ LEGAL OBLIGATIONS

If you are doing commissions don't do anything until you get a signed contract. Why? Because there is so much at stake due to the fact that you are selling an idea and not a finished product. It is true that you need to produce a finished work of art before you are paid in full, but there is a lot of process involved before it is completed.

Most contracts have three distinct stages. The first is:

The Proposal Stage

This is the point where you as the craftsperson meet with the client to explain and demonstrate your work. If the prospective commission came through an architect, interior designer or art consultant, that person will attend this initial meeting. If you are dealing directly with the client or a committee, you are on your own. As the result of this meeting and similar meetings with other applicants you will or will not get the nod to go ahead with the project.

A letter of agreement is signed by both you and the client for the preliminary study only. The letter of agreement (or contract if you wish) obligates the client to pay you to research and design a model for the proposed commission. The fee may vary from $250 to $2500 or more depending on the scale of the project. But it is understood that this fee is for the preliminary study only and that regardless of whether the design is approved by the client or not, you will receive your fee as stated in the contract. With a signed agreement in hand you proceed to measure, sketch, photograph, and get any other information you need about the space.

Your objective at this stage is to make a drawing, scale model, collage or whatever to show the client and/or agent what you propose to make. The more thorough your presentation the better chance you have of getting the go-ahead for the actual commission, so you should specify what materials you will be using and why, how long it will take you to complete the projects, when you can begin the project and your charges.

When you have completed your study you are ready to meet with the client again and explain what it is that you are going to do for them. You are ready for the:

Presentation Contract

This is where your selling skills are really put to the test. Remember that you are the expert, so give them the impression that you have really done your homework. The client will have many, many questions but you will be prepared because you have already asked yourself the same questions and have answers to them. If you are working with an agent it is an excellent idea to get together before you meet with the client to go over your presentation to iron out any bugs that may exist. Here are the points that you should cover in your presentation.

1. Show the model or sketch of the proposed work.
2. Explain, in detail, why this particular design meets their specific needs.
3. Specify the material you will be using and why.
4. Itemize the cost of the materials, labor, research installation and overhead.
5. Present the contract to the client.

This is not the time to gloss over anything or try to rush through an explanation. Take as much time as you need to explain your proposal and answer all the client's questions. When you feel the client understands what you propose and has had all his questions answered, present the contract.

The contract will simply state in written (and legal) form what you have already reviewed in your presentation. Each contract will have slight variations but all should include the following agreements:

1. The client shall not alter or cause the work to be damaged in any way.
2. If the work or its installation is found to be defective due to the artist's fault within one year, you will replace or repair it.
3. Delivery or completion times are based on receipt of payment. The contract should not say, "The project will be started within 30 days of July 31," but would say instead, "The project will be started within 30 days of the receipt of payment for 50% of the total agreed-upon cost of the project."

Do not start your work until the client has honored his obligation to pay you 50% of the total fee to get you started.

You have made your presentation and the contract is in the client's hands. What do you do now? Well, you wait for the client to sign the contract so you can get on with the commission. Remember that this is a business transaction and you must protect your interests. Keep these three points in mind:

1. Always have the contract prepared and ready to sign at the Presentation Contract Conference. If you don't you may lose the commission.
2. Ask the client(s) to sign upon presentation but don't be surprised if they don't. Frequently, they will want their lawyers to review the document before signing. If they ask for time to think about it, agree, but set a time limitation of no more than 30 days.
3. Remind them that you are prepared to start the project upon the signing of the contract and receipt of 50% of the commission amount.

Contract Consummation Stage

This is the most exciting stage because you are able to see the completed piece installed and you receive payment for the remaining half of the commission amount. This is also the time when preplanning and exact contract specification pay off.

Contracts exist for one reason only, to see that the parties involved live up to their agreed obligations. In this particular instance, you are agreeing to perform a certain task for a certain consideration (money) from the client. The more specific the contract is the better chance you have of receiving payment upon completion of your task. In other words, if you can prove that you did what was specified in the contract you have fulfilled your obligation and now the client must do the same (pay).

In most cases the closing contract is part of the original contract but regardless of how and where it appears it must be signed by both parties at the completion of the commission. The closing contract in essence transfers ownership of the commissioned piece from you to the client. It also puts you in a much better position because the client now has to prove negligence or deception on your part in order to collect damages.

I cannot emphasize enough the importance of getting everything in writing. You should consult your lawyer to insure that your first contract is legal and binding. Once you have a legal form, you can use the same format for other commissions you undertake which are similar. If you negotiate a completely new deal go back to your attorney and construct a new contract.

□   DEVELOPING COMMISSION SALES

Experience counts, in commission work more than anywhere else. My advice is to get one commission (even if you have to do it for the cost of materials only) and keep building. If your first commission is for a church, immediately contact other churches and make appointments to show your work. If you started in a small church, contact larger ones. You need to be aggressive! If you just completed a mural for a city library how about sending news releases to the head of the state library system and anyone else associated with libraries. Send news releases to newspapers and library-related magazines to let as many people know about the project as possible.

It's hard to believe that there is any one thing that craftsmen hate more than bookkeeping. But there is! It is selling oneself. At every marketing seminar I conduct the majority of the people attending express their great dislike of selling themselves and their work. I know how they feel because selling is not one of my favorite activities either, but it has to be done if you intend to make a living from crafts. Sure, you can hire someone to do it for you, but in many market channels it doesn't work. In commissions you *have* to do the selling either to the client directly or to the agent.

A technique that I use might help. I know that the success of my business depends on continued contacts with business and professional people so I schedule a specific time each week when I get on the phone or at the typewriter and make my contacts for that week. My studio is only a few feet away but I stay out until I have accomplished the objectives that I have established for myself for that day. When it's complete I can breath a sigh of relief, feel a great sense of accomplishment and get to work in the studio. Try it, it works.

There is an old saying that it's not always the best person who gets the job, it's usually the best person known about at the time. Let people know that you exist. Every bit of publicity you can generate will help you when you present your ideas to your clients.

Memberships in professional organizations also help tremendously. Become a member or a subscriber to one of the journals for interior designers or other areas that interest you to keep up with the latest developments in the field. The magazine or newsletter may, for example, announce that Acme Interiors, Inc. was just awarded the contract to do the inside of the new Prudential Building in Tallahassee. Now's the time to contact them and show them what you can do. Use your imagination but by all means keep active and keep your name in the news. Everything helps.

☐   IS THIS THE RIGHT MARKET FOR YOU?

The crafts business is extremely diverse and what fits one person does not fit another. Generally speaking commissions are not for production craftsmen. Having said that, I must immediately cite some exceptions. Production weavers, potters and other craftsmen frequently get commissions to design and produce a coordinated set of table runners, placemats or stoneware dinnerware. But these commissions are fairly rare. Just about all the craftsmen I know who are doing commissions are doing them on a full time basis. In other words, they have chosen commissions as their exclusive crafts marketing channel.

I have been emphasizing through this book that making crafts is a business and you need to have a good business sense to survive. It's probably more true in commission sales than in any other crafts area. You are dealing with big business and you need to demonstrate that you know what you are doing.

A respected interior designer pointed out that people in his profession are always looking for trends and they like to work with craftspeople who keep up with the trends. I can hear some craftspeople protesting "I do what I want to do with my crafts, not what is trendy." That's fine with me but I hope you have a rich uncle, because if you are not responsive to what people want to buy you are not going to sell.

Through all this you need to concentrate on keeping your own style. People will contact you and will contract with you because they like what you do. If you make the mistake of being too trendy, you'll give the impression of blowing with the wind and nobody will hire you. Yes, it is a balancing act between keeping your own style and meeting the client's needs but any creative process is an evolutionary one and it is possible to be responsive to your clients and maintain your own artistic integrity.

□ GETTING OUT

You have the right to stop doing commission work any time you want. But it is absolutely essential that you honor any contracts currently in progress. Some commissions take a year or two to complete so try to keep that time span in mind. If you have done the preliminary study and have been paid for it but find you cannot complete the project, you should offer to refund the fee for the preliminary study. If the client elects not to proceed with the project then you may legally and morally keep the fee for the study. Remember that this is a personal business and clients and agents talk with other clients and agents. Questionable business practices on your part will spread quickly and you'll have difficulty obtaining additional commissions.

□ MARKETING HIGHLIGHTS FOR COMMISSIONS

1. Commissions can be financially rewarding if you plan effectively from the start.
2. Don't promise what you can't deliver.
3. Dress the part of a successful businessman to bridge the artist/businessman gap.
4. Make sure that you are aware of all the hidden costs in estimating the cost for a commission.
5. Develop your unique style but let your clients know that you are responsive to their needs and wants.
6. It is up to you to make contacts with people who are in a position to award contracts.
7. Everyone gets turned down. The craftspeople who keep trying get the commissions.
8. Your portfolio must be professionally done. If you are not an accomplished photographer have a professional do it for you.

Please! This is not an area to try to save money.

9. The cold approach is not as effective as the warm approach but they both work and both should be used.

10. Have a professional vita and photos of your work neatly packaged so that you can leave it with prospective clients.

11. This is a personal marketing channel. Use your contact whenever possible.

12. Listen to what your client's wants and needs are before you start shooting your big mouth off.

13. Specify in detail in the contract what you will and will not do.

14. Proceed step-by-step. Do not go to the next stage until you are paid for work already performed and have a signed agreement for the next stage from your client.

15. Corporate and government commissions can get mired in red tape but if you persevere they can be rewarding.

16. Get everything in writing and make sure they are legal documents. You are dealing in ideas in commission work and there's always the danger of the client pulling out because "that's not what he had in mind at all."

17. Success breeds more success. Make sure people know that you have successfully completed previous commissions and it will be much easier getting new ones.

18. Keep records of your commissions and use them as sales tools for future contracts.

Chapter 16

Mail Order Marketing

Mail order marketing is the fastest growing marketing channel in the country because it offers convenient and easy shopping for the buyer and for the seller.

Mail order marketing can be very lucrative or you can lose your shirt. Remember the pet rock? Much of the millions of dollars of sales were generated through mail order. Obviously you don't hear about unsuccessful mail order marketing attempts but there are many.

Unfortunately, many wild claims have been made about mail order business and get-rich-quick schemes abound, but if you proceed cautiously and systematically, mail order is a profitable way to market your crafts. The secret is to start small, build on your successes and minimize your losses. You can be assured that there will be some failures; even people who have been selling via mail order for years have their failures, but make up for them with their successes.

☐ THE THREE TYPES OF MAIL ORDER MARKETING

The people in the mail order business are very creative and have come up with many different ways to advertise their products, but all of them fall under one of three main categories: classified advertising, display advertising, and direct mail. I have left out television and radio because they have little application to the craft business.

Classified Advertising

This is the easiest and cheapest way to get started. We all see classified ads in the daily paper, indeed nearly everyone has placed a classified at one time or another. The ad is placed under the appropriate heading such as boats, cars, garage sales, help wanted, etc. The fee for the ad is based on the number of words used and the number of times the ad is run. Most mail order advertisers don't use newspapers, because they are thrown away daily. They want something more lasting — like a magazine.

Examine classified ads, you will see that some describe an item and ask for money while others offer to send you more information. These two ad types are called, respectively, one-step and two-step ads.

The classified ad that asks for money is a one-step ad because they tell you about their product and ask you to send money to receive it. Here is an example:

> Hand-made weather vane, solid brass, rooster theme.
> Easily mounted. Satisfaction Guaranteed. $95. Vane
> Master; 1268 Smithfield Road; Swamp Creek, VA 30681

This type of ad usually receives very little response. Why? Would you send $95 for an item that you had never seen, made by someone you don't know, living in a state that is 1800 miles from you? No, you wouldn't, and most other people wouldn't either. That's why most classified ads are the two-step type. Here is an example:

> Hand-made weather vanes. Solid brass, twelve different
> designs, free catalog. Vane Master; 1268 Smithfield Road;
> Swamp Creek, VA 30681

Would you send for more information? If you were at all interested in weather vanes, I'm sure you would. What have you got to lose? For the cost of a postage stamp you can get more information on these weather vanes and make up your mind at your leisure.

If you were using a two-step ad to sell your products you would mail out a complete description of your product to any who responds to your ad. The descriptive materials are your real selling tools. The classified ad is only used to get people who are mildly interested in your product to send for more information.

Display Advertising

You see these everywhere. They advertise a product by showing a picture accompanied by a small amount of text. Cigarette ads, liquor ads, car ads, clothing ads — all are display ads.

Some are just reminders that the product has desirable features that you should sample the next time you are at the store. The ads listed above fall into this category.

Other display ads come under the one- or two-step classification. The ad below is an example of a one-step display ad. Note that it

has a picture, price and address. It is designed to give you enough information about the product that you may want to buy it. This particular ad was positioned to attract craft shop and gallery owners.

The next display ad is a two-step ad. It tells you a little about the product and offer to provide more detailed information free.

What's the advantage of a display ad over a classified? In most cases you get a higher response because it is seen by more people, plus display ads are often placed in more favorable locations in the magazines so that they are seen more often. Veteran mail order advertisers specify that the ads be run on the odd numbered pages. Why? Because as you open the magazine you see the right hand page (the odd numbered ones) first.

Direct Mail

If you have ever bought anything on credit, have a charge card, belong to an organization or subscribe to a magazine, your name is on a mailing list or two. Your name, along with millions of others, is bought and sold by mail order companies over and over again. This is all part of the country's multi-billion dollar direct mail industry. There are hundreds of list brokers who sell lists of people interested in specific products, whether art materials, antiques, x-rated films, cars, food or skin diving. With the advent of the computer any good-sized broker can custom design a list for you. For example if you want a list of female executives between the ages of 30 and 55 making over $35,000 a year who are gourmet cooks and have bought something via direct mail during the last year you could get one. It's even possible, using zip codes, to get lists for people in a specific geographical area.

You can rent names either from list brokers or directly from magazine publishers or credit card companies. It may surprise you to know that research shows that a very high percentage of direct mail pieces do get opened and read. The people responding, however, falls to a much lower level: 2% is considered "good."

Each of the three marketing methods will be discussed in more detail later in this chapter and you'll even find out how to off-set your advertising costs by renting out the names of the people responding to your ads. But before you get too excited, you need to take an objective look at:

☐ MAIL ORDER: PROMISE AND PITFALLS

Mail order marketing has the potential for making you rich very quickly, and it does happen, just as people win at horseracing or lottery games. Like horseracing, however, mail order marketing is a gamble and the more you know about the business the better your chances of winning become. The secret to mail order marketing is having the right product at the right price with the *right advertising.*

The most requested topic at my marketing seminars is mail order marketing. Why? Because people are impressed with numbers and the potential for profit. When I tell them *Yankee Magazine* has a monthly readership of three million, is a proven winner in mail order sales, and lets you run an ad for as little as $60, there is almost total silence as everyone mentally calculates how much money they can make from a single ad if only 2% of the people respond. Before you get carried away, here are the facts.

Advantages

The principal advantage is that you can put your message in front of a lot of people. Instead of having one or two people stop at your craft booth every once-in-a-while, you can tell thousands, even millions of people what you make. There is an old saying that if you tell enough people about your product eventually someone will buy it no matter what it is. One likes to think that advertising is more systematic than that but the principle still holds true.

Mail order marketing allows you to be the retailer. You can be the manufacturer and the seller, so you can get the full retail price rather than selling wholesale to galleries and shops.

There is very little overhead. All you need is a desk, a typewriter, some paper and envelopes and you're in the mail order business. Naturally, you'll need boxes and shipping materials to send your products out, but even that's not a major undertaking.

There is potential for high demand and, thus, high profit, but you've got to be able to meet the demand.

You can do everything from your studio. There is no need to travel, rent a shop or anything else. Just make your craft item and fill orders.

Disadvantages

Results from your ads are often disappointing. It's tempting to say, "Gee, *Yankee Magazine* has a readership of 3,000,000. If I place an ad for my toys and only 2% of the people respond, that's still 60,000 responses. That will keep me busy for five years." The truth is that responses are difficult to predict. So much depends on your ad, the time of the year, the economy, etc. Most mail order experts agree that if the ad pays for itself the first time you should go ahead and insert another ad.

Ads are expensive! Small display ads are often $500 and up. The *National Enquirer* claims a weekly circulation of five million and charges $14,000 for a full-page ad run one time. I won't even tell you what an ad in *Better Homes and Gardens* costs. If an ad costs $1,000, you're going to have to sell a lot of honey jars, leather wallets, or placemats to make ends meet.

It takes at least two months before you get any results because most magazines have a lead time of at least 60 days for ads. If you want to attract the Christmas buyers, you'll need to aim for the November issue, which means that the ad and your payment must be received by the magazine in August. When you see the typical Christmas in July sales in the local department stores, you'd better get going on your ad copy!

It's impossible to predict what will and what will not sell. You need to test to see what works best. This can take some time and be expensive.

There are strict governmental regulations regarding mail order. One of the most important is that you must ship an order within thirty days. If you are unable to do so, you must notify the customer in writing and must offer a full refund if the customer desires it.

It takes a long time to get the business established, particularly if you start small and expand slowly (which is the only way to do it.) Don't expect to make a profit in the beginning. Start up costs will wipe out any profit you make; be content with a break-even status for the first few months. Successful mail order businesses are based on repeat sales.

Mail order has, because of unscrupulous advertisers, had some bad press and people are cautious about mail-order claims. This fact, combined with the volume of so-called "junk mail" can reduce your chances of success in mail order. The solution is to be absolutely honest in your dealings and prove to your customers that regardless of what they believe about mail order, at least you deliver what you promise.

□ COMPETITION

In the mail order business, competition is good for you. In fact, if you can't find any competition you may want to think twice about trying your product in mail order. Why? Because ads that are repeated month after month are successful, otherwise they would not be repeated (remember how costly they are). Looking at the competition is an excellent way to begin your research. answer their ads and look at their material. Does it make you want to buy? Can you make as good a product for the same price? Can you offer better services, a wider selection, a faster response? Analyze their entire advertising system and see how they have done it. You already know a little about the types of ads, so take note of whether it is a classified or display ad, one-step or two-step, and what type of heading they used. Did the ad promise something that was unique, cheaper, better, not available anywhere else, etc.? What was it that attracted your attention?

There is absolutely nothing wrong with analyzing another person's ad. All mail order advertisers do it. Obviously, you can't copy their ads, but you can learn from them. If you have a few moments you might look at different ads for similar items and see how similar the ads really are.

An interesting thing happens that I feel can be a benefit to you when you start your mail order advertising campaign (if you decide that this is a marketing area for you). Once your ad appears you'll get lots of ads from other mail order advertisers. A lot of it will be junk, but some if it will be very good. Save the ads and look at them to glean ideas for your own.

☐   ENTERING THE MARKET

At the beginning of this chapter I recommended that you study successful mail order businesses and use their success as a model for yours. Let's take a proven ad used by Design Group to see just why it is profitable.

The Ad

Sal Villano, the owner of Design Group has a variety of ads which he uses in different magazines. Each one is a little different but keeps the same basic style so the ad is recognized as belonging to Design Group. Naturally each ad is coded so that he can keep track of the number of responses from each magazine. In the example shown the key is Dept-C. If he wanted to know the issue of the magazine that produced the most response he could add a month key (Dept-CJ, for *Crafts*, January Issue).

The Cost

The ad asks for $1.00 for a catalog (refunded with first order). This is effective because $1.00 is a very small amount, it's easy to slip into an envelope and mail, and while it reduces the number of responses somewhat, the people who do respond are serious buyers because they have already risked $1.00. The rule in mail order is that you can ask for up to $5.00 in a one-step classified and up to $10.00 in a small display, so Design Group is well within the guidelines.

The Follow Up
People who mail in their $1.00 receive a 32-page catalog of plans, thus meeting two of the cardinal mail order rules:

1. You must offer the customer a choice of products
2. You must depend on repeat business for your profit

Plus, Sal Villano has two other things going for him that help to make his mail order business a success. He has a product that is low priced ($3 — $5) and that is not readily available elsewhere.

Mail order marketing principals work with other products and other ads. But for now let's see how you go about:

☐ CHOOSING THE RIGHT MAIL ORDER MARKET

You already know about competition and how it is good for you in mail order. The best rule for craftspeople getting started in mail orders is to imitate success and that's why I analyzed the Design Group. If you want to exercise your creative energies and try mail order marketing your own way, go right ahead. Just don't ask anyone to bail you out. Others have made enough mistakes and spent enough of their own money finding what marketing techniques work. You should first identify who is selling crafts through mail order and how they are doing it. You do that by conducting a little research.

☐ RULE NUMBER ONE

Identify a number of magazines that have shop-by-mail sections and classified advertising sections. For our purposes, we will discuss classified ads as this is the best way to begin. If your ads work well, you can expand into display ads later. Your research is best done in a good library which maintains a large subscription list.

Take a notebook and pencil and plan to spend some time browsing through magazines. Look through as many current magazine issues as you can and simply note each ad for a craft item. You list will look something like this:

Hand Carved Signs — *Yankee*, October, 1984
Stoneware Candle Lanterns — *Southern Living*, October 1984
Printed Fabrics — *Better Homes and Gardens*, September 1984
etc.

Continue making your list until you have a good long one. Then look through the back issues of the same magazines to see if the same ads appeared three to six months ago. If they did, then you can be absolutely sure the ads are profitable. Then condense your list to those that have been repeated and are, therefore, profitable.

Next look at all the repeat ads and see what makes them effective. Do they offer free information, personalized service, hard-to-get items, something new or improved?

The president of a political polling service observed that successful politicians all had the same ability to appeal to three feelings in people: emotion, emotion and emotion. The same holds true in advertising. Check to see that your ad appeals to people's emotions, that it promises to help them in a specific way. Remember one of the basic tenets of marketing is that a customer buys something that satisfies his wants or needs, not yours. So the first rule is to develop a good ad, based on already successful ads, that fills the wants and needs of a customer.

□ RULE NUMBER TWO

Advertise your crafts only in magazines with large shop-by-mail sections. Contrary to popular belief, competition is good for you! People who buy magazines with large mail order sections do so because they shop by mail and want the best selection they can get. They look forward to finding out what new products are available. I can almost guarantee that you'll lose your shirt if you advertise in a magazine that has a readership not accustomed to mail order. Would you go to a pet shop to buy a used car?

□ RULE NUMBER THREE

Select magazines whose readership is interested in your product. This sounds obvious, but many craftspeople get so involved in their work they believe that anyone who sees their work will automatically reach for their purse and buy. When they see that their ad will reach three million people, visions of trucks, backing up to their studios delivering more supplies so that they can keep up with the demand become common. There is no accurate way of predicting what your ad will generate, but the response is generally higher in a specialized magazine like *Creative Crafts* than in a general magazine like the *Saturday Evening Post*.

□ RULE NUMBER FOUR

Lastly, test, test, test! This is the only way. Start with a small classified ad and wait for the results. Some mail order experts recommend running at least three or four ads before assessing results because people will respond better if they know they are dealing with an established business. I have nothing against repeating ads, but I think you should start with one. If an ad is good, it will work the first time. If it's bad there is no sense in repeating it.

The two-step ad is always the best approach unless your price is very low ($5 or less). I learned my lesson the hard way when I placed a classified ad in a magazine with a readership of 3,000,000. I used a one-step ad for a product costing $10. The ad cost me $85.00

and I received three responses. I ran a two-step ad for the same product in a magazine with half the circulation, and at half the price. This ad drew 137 inquiries and 13 final sales.

Let's assume that you have your ad written and are ready to try it in a magazine or two. How do you select the magazine in which to try it? If you did your research thoroughly you won't be making your decision completely in the dark. The best magazines to advertise in are the special interest magazines because they give the best buy for your advertising dollar. For example, *The Saturday Evening Post* has a certified readership of 559,234 per month and charges $2.60 a word for classified advertising. *Decorating and Craft Ideas* has a readership of 1,000,000 and charges the same rate for classified ads. The difference is *Decorating and Craft Ideas* has a readership of people interested in the crafts exclusively whereas maybe 10% of the *Post's* readership is interested in the crafts. So, for the same advertising dollar you are reaching 1,000,000 interested people in one magazine and 55,923 in the other.

There are two fundamental methods to help you select the best magazines in which to advertise your crafts, and both work equally well. In my many years working with craftsmen, I know they are a very creative and individualistic bunch, so I'll let you choose the method that works best for you.

□ METHOD A

Make a list of groups that would be interested in your craft. Your list might include working mothers, antique collectors, camping enthusiasts, and ten other groups. Take your list to the local library and study the *Reader's Guide to Periodical Literature Subject Guide*. This is a list of every article published in magazines, organized by subject. Your objective is to find magazines that are read by the people you have listed as being interested in your crafts. Let's say that you see in the *Subject Guide* an article entitled "Mothers Organize to Restore Historical Building." This gives you a clue that the readers of this magazine might be interested in your stencil designs so you look at the *Subject Guide* and see that the article appeared in *Antiques Monthly*, October, 1982 issue. Your next step is to look through several issues of that magazine to see if anyone else has crafts advertised. If they have you have a magazine that has marketing potential for you.

□ METHOD B

Do just the opposite! Go directly to the *Reader's Guide to Periodical Literature Subject Guide* and look through the subject categories and jot down the ones that interest you. After you have reviewed and edited your list look up the articles published on the subjects you have listed and record the names of the magazines they were published in.

One other reference you should consult before selecting the magazine(s) you want to use is the *Standard Rate and Data Reference;*

5201 Old Skokie Orchard Road; Skokie, IL 60076, $40.00. This guide lists the advertising rates for all magazines published in North America. The listings also contain a profile of the readership of each magazine which can be very helpful in choosing your population. For example, the entry for *Antiques Monthly* advises that its readers are in the upper income bracket, an average age of 45, and live predominately in urban areas. In some cases there will be information on what percentage of the readership responded to ads last year and how much they spent. The more information you have about your potential customers the better off you'll be. If you cannot get all the information you wish from the references listed write to the advertising offices of the magazines you are interested in and ask for their rate card and reader demographics. They will gladly furnish this information in the form of a rate card which also informs you of the last day an ad will be accepted for any particular issue. The rate card may read like this: Ads due 15th of 2nd., which translates into: all advertisements are due with payment by the fifteenth of the month two months before the publication month. As an example, the deadline for the ads for the April issue is February 15th. Remember that it takes about two months before your ad appears. It is evident that you will have to plan well ahead as to when you want to try to stimulate your sales using the mail order channel.

□   MARKETING STRATEGIES

You've done all the research and have written and re-written your ad at least fifty times. There's only one thing left to do: take action. Choose the best magazine, type your ad, specify what category you want it placed in, write your check and send it all in to the magazine. In a week or so you'll receive confirmation of receipt and the category and issue in which the ad will appear. All you do now is wait, the hardest part of mail order marketing.

People ask me what kind of response they can expect. That's impossible to predict, but you can estimate the total response you'll get shortly after the ad appears. The rule is that you can expect 60% of your total responses within 30 days of issuance and about 90% by the end of eight weeks. You'll continue to get responses to your ads years after, but they'll just be a trickle. Naturally you've keyed your ad so you know which ad people responded to. I ran an ad in *McCall's Needlework and Crafts* over two years ago and still get responses. I know what ad they are responding to because of the key I used.

We've discussed the potential of mail order and I'm sure you've made plans to handle the orders as they come in, but what if you don't get any orders? Sometimes ads simply don't work. I've been at this so long that I can look at a page of classifieds and pick out the ads that don't work. I'm not always right and I still write a bad ad now and then, but all things considered, my batting average is pretty good. If your ad doesn't work there are three area that you need to check:

      1. Does the ad excite you? Would you respond to such as ad if you saw it in a magazine? If your answer is no, you'll need to

rewrite your ad.

2. Is it in the right category in the classified section? Are there ads similar to yours in the same section? If not, see if there is a better category.

3. Are you advertising in the right magazine? If you're the only one advertising hand-lettered birth certificates in *Playboy*, perhaps you chose the wrong magazine.

The secret to success is to test, test and test again. Remember the secret of crafts marketing, "Try something! If it works, do more of it. If it doesn't, try something else." The ad you run is the key to your success and failure. Let me give you a personal example. When I first started in mail order I was selling a crafts marketing book that I had published myself. I placed an ad in *The Mother Earth News* that read:

CASH IN YOUR HANDS! Handicrafters sell everything you make.
I do. Complete guide $10. . . .and my address.

This didn't do well at all because people were reluctant to send $10 for something they knew nothing about.

Another ad placed in a monthly magazine did better but not great. It read:

Handicrafters, Hobbyists, Sell everything you make.
Free details, SASE. . . .and my address.

I found that asking for a self addressed stamped envelope (SASE) seriously cut back on my responses. I also discovered that quite a few people didn't know what a SASE was because a number of the responses I got were addressed to SASE; . . . .and then my address.

I finally hit on the fact that most craftspeople depend on crafts for only part of their income, particularly the readers of the magazines I was advertising in. I changed the ad to read:

Earn Extra Money selling your handicrafts.
Fantastic demand, high profits. Free details.

This ad works well and keeps on working.

You might be interested in knowing that there are some words that have been proven to be the most effective in advertising. They are FREE, NEW, MONEY, LIMITED TIME, EXCLUSIVE, IMPROVED and RICHES.

When you have a proven winner by all means try a display ad. But I don't recommend a display ad until you have gotten good response from a number of your classified ads.

□   DIRECT MAIL

Most mail order experts feel that direct mail campaigns offer the most profitable avenue for maximum sales. Why? You have the most control in direct mail because you can design your advertisement for a specific group of people, can present your complete story to them and can be assured that a high percentage of the people receiving your materials will at least look at it. I do not recommend a direct mail campaign until you have tested your product through classified ads and display ads. You need to prove a product through classified ads and display ads. You need to have a product that will sell before you spend money developing a direct mail campaign.

I'd like also to recommend *Elephants in the Mailbox* by Roger Horchow, published by Time Books. Roger Horchow has a very successful mail order business. In his book he describes how he got to where he is today by making lots of mistakes. The book is enjoyable to read and informative at the same time.

The Direct Mail Package

When you send a direct mail package keep in mind that you have one chance to convince the customer to buy. Therefore, if your package is to attract the customer's interest, tell him about the uniqueness of your product, how it can benefit him and provide an easy way for the customer to order your product. The first thing you start with is:

The sales letter. All of us are creatures of habit and when we open an envelope we expect to see a letter. Include a headline designed to attract the customer's attention, use letterhead stationery and a salutation such as "Dear Friend." Remember that your letter is a personal appeal so that it should look like and read like a letter. That means the letter should be typed and not printed. It helps if the letter is broken up so that it attracts the customer from a visual standpoint. The craftsmanship and aesthetic appeal of the letter is as important as any craft product you make.

The letter should be two to four pages long, depending on how much you want to tell the customer about your product and should close with an action statement such as: "I want you to try this widget at absolutely no risk to you. Each widget is backed by our exclusive money back guarantee, if you order now. Send today, or for immediate service call our toll free number at 800-123-456-7899."

The Order form. This works best if it is printed on a separate piece of paper. Restate the guarantee and the sales agreement and include an action statement on the order form such as: "Yes! Send me my no risk widget. I understand that if I am not completely satisfied I can return if for a full refund if I do so within 30 days. Enclosed is my $19.95."

Give them the opportunity to charge their purchase using either MasterCard or Visa.

The return envelope. You want to make it as easy as possible for the customer to buy. If the customer has to find an envelope, address it and stick a stamp on it he may not buy. It's much easier to simply slide the order form in a return envelope already addressed and slip it in the nearest mail box.

List Brokers

List brokers are more than willing to help you. Particularly if you are just getting started in this market channel. Tell them what type of audience you want to appeal to and they will find you the list that is best for you. This service is free as long as you rent your names from them. Rental rates do differ but most run around $60 per thousand. Always try to rent around 2,000 names for your test. This sampling will give you a good indication as to whether your direct mail package is working.

List brokers can be found in the yellow pages of larger cities under the category of Mailing Lists. Like any good profession, list brokers have a professional organization that polices their members. If a list broker is a member of the DMMA you can feel confident of their professional abilities. The *Standard Rate and Data Service* mentioned earlier in this chapter publishes the *Direct Mail List and Data Guide,* containing over 25,000 different lists. If you can't find a few good lists in that lot perhaps your product is so unique that you are the only one who likes it.

Renting or Selling Lists

You can earn some extra money if you can work out a deal with a list broker to buy your list. Sometimes he will want to exchange lists with you and that can be beneficial as well. Contact a list broker with whom you have done business when you have accumulated a list of 5,000 or more names. Make sure the list is of people who have bought your product, not just people who have enquired.

☐ OTHER MAIL ORDER MARKETS

Other than the traditional markets in mail order in which you become the advertiser, shipper, retailer and manufacturer, you may want to explore making crafts for mail order companies. Mail order is one of the fastest growing marketing areas in the country and everybody seems to be getting in on it. Airlines give each passenger a mail order catalog to read (and hopefully order from), the major oil companies offer mail order bargains with each statement, as do department stores when they mail out monthly statements to their customers.

There are two ways that you can provide crafts for mail order firms. One is to wholesale to them directly and the other is to agree to a drop-ship arrangement. Wholesaling accounts may be developed by you directly or you may be approached by a buyer at a wholesale show. I have already reviewed wholesale selling techniques in the chapter on The Wholesale Show so I won't go into detail here. There are two references that you may be interested in looking at. Both will provide you with the names of companies that are in the mail order business. The *Mail Order Business Directory* is available from B. Klein Publications, Coral Springs, Florida, 33065 and contains 7,500 names and addresses of mail order firms. Another reference entitled *Department Stores and Mail Order Firms* lists 1,000 mail order companies and is available form Business Guides, Inc. 425 Park Avenue, New York, New York 10022.

You may be asked to drop ship your craft items particularly if they are large. Drop shipping means that the order is placed with the mail order firm but the actual item is shipped from the place of manufacturer. Let's say that you make large wooden chests inlaid with whale bone. A mail order company wants to feature your chest in their next catalog and you agree to supply them with chests at a stated price. Remember that if the agreement is for drop shipping you will ship directly to the customer from your studio so figure your packing and shipping costs into your wholesale price.

The mail order company assumes all the responsibility for the printing and mailing of the catalog. When a customer orders a chest from the catalog for let's say $500 the company acknowledges the order, sends you a check for $300 (your agreed upon price for the chest and shipping) and you send the chest directly to the customer.

Another suggestion. Buy something through mail order and in a short period of time you will begin receiving catalogs from other mail order companies because they will have rented your name for a list broker. If you receive a catalog that interests you and contains craft items at about the same retail price as your work you might be interested in contacting them about selling your work.

☐   HOW TO START YOUR OWN AD AGENCY

When you first start out in mail order the best advice is to mail in your check with your ad. Later, if you find that mail order is a market channel that you find profitable you might consider opening your own in-house agency. There are several advantages and it's a good way to save money.

Most craftspeople do all their own ad planning, paste-up and other services that an ad agency normally performs. Therefore, you may legally call yourself an ad agency and claim the 15% discount that all ad agencies get. Your reaction may be "Fifteen per cent is not much. Why should I bother?" Well fifteen per cent can add up to a rather substantial amount when your advertising budget reaches $10,000 per year. In addition to the 15% you can save on each ad placed you can save an additional 2% by paying cash with the ad. When you begin you won't be able to do this but as soon as you have established an account with a magazine and have established your own in-house agency you can automatically take 15% off the gross and an additional 2% off the net for prompt payment — a savings of almost 17%.

I suggest that if you do establish your own in-house ad agency you have a different address for it. You may want to use your studio address for your crafts business and a box number for your ad agency. This may not be necessary, but some magazines will refuse to grant an agency discount if the business name and ad agency name and address is the same.

If you do decide to establish you own ad agency I suggest you consult a good reference book on mail order marketing. One that I recommend is *How to Get Rich in Mail Order* by Melvin Powers, Wilshire Publishing. It is a step-by-step guide with stories about how people have made money through mail order.

□   PRICING

The rule of thumb in mail order marketing is that your selling price should be six times your actual cost. If it's not, don't even bother to try mail order. Why such a high mark-up? Advertising and mailing costs are going to eat up a lot of your profits. If your mark-up is ten times your cost you'll be in even better shape.

Here's an actual example. A full page ad in a magazine with a circulation of 150,000 brought a .0016% response for a total of 250 orders. The ad was for a book priced at $12.95. The book cost $1 each to print, plus another $1 each for shipping and handling. The ad cost $820. If we figure the costs, $820 for the ad and $2 for each book for printing and mailing, we get a figure of $1320. The actual amount of money taken in was $3237.50 (250 times $12.95) for a profit of $1917.50. Note that the cost of the item sold was 13 times the actual cost. This is fairly easy to do in the book business, but much more difficult to do in crafts. What's the solution? Watch your costs and plan on follow-up sales.

Little details make the difference in mail orders. A half cent difference per page on printing costs doesn't seem like much but when you have 10,000 flyers printed up it's a difference of $500 and that could easily be the difference between making a profit or not.

Keep track of each ad and the results so that you can tell if you are making a profit or not. I recommend that you buy a spiral notebook and use one page for each ad. Here's what it might look like:

Publication___ Crafts Review_____

Ad Copy_____ Free! Hand-made toy catalog. Kids love them. Unique,_____

_____ Personalized,Love Made Toys, Inc. Box 747 CR Wareham,_____

_____ Massachusetts 02571_____

_____

Issue__ November_____ On Sale____ October 15_____

Cost of Ad___ $30.00_____Category__ Craft items for sale_____

Results_____

_____

Date Received	Number Received	Total
10/15	5	5
10/18	12	17
10/19	4	21
10/20	3	24
10/21	7	31
10/24	15	46
10/25	18	64
10/29	10	74
11/1	5	79
11/2	12	91
11/3	1	92
11/5	0	92
11/6	2	94
11/10	3	97
11/12	2	99
11/17	1	100

The example chosen is for a classified two-step ad. Let's say that you received 100 letters of inquiry, your follow-up information was sent out immediately and you received a 20% response. With an average sale of $20, your total income was $400. From this you must deduct your costs as follows.

Ad (20 words @ $1.50/word)	$ 30.00
Postage (for 100 letters)	$ 20.00
Brochures (100 @ 25¢/brochure)	$ 25.00
Craft Costs (20 @ $2.00/item)	$ 40.00
Postage (20 @ $2.00/package)	$ 40.00
Overhead/handling ($2.00 per package)	$ 40.00
Total	$195.00
Total Profit (Income minus expenses)	$285.00

If this is your profit picture, I suggest you go ahead and expand your ads to other magazines and run the original ad again in the same magazine. Be sure that you use a key so you know where your response is coming from. The key in our example is CR. If you put your key right next to your box number or street address, i.e., Box 747CR or 1234CR Parkwood Drive you don't get charged for another word.

The success of any mail order operation depends on volume. All your printing costs are much cheaper in volume and bulk mailing permits save you lots of money. Check with the local post office to see what the regulations are about special mailing rates. Keep track of your costs and if you find out that you are not making money find out why. It's really very simple; you need to concentrate on keeping your costs to a minimum and your income to a maximum. Remember that some products are not right for mail orders and nobody has all the answers. Even mail order experts test and test until they either get it right or discover that it was a bad idea in the first place.

□   LEGAL OBLIGATIONS

When you enter the mail order market you not only make yourself known to a lot more people but also come under the scrutiny of agencies of federal, state and local governments. The Federal Trade Commission and the United States Postal Service are going to be interested in your operation. State and local agencies are going to be interested in possibilities of fraud, the way you handle sales transactions, etc., etc. There really is nothing to fear as long as you are operating legally and are selling what you are advertising.

You are obligated by law to fill orders within 30 days or notify the customer why you cannot. If you cannot fill the order within the required time you must offer the customer a full refund. If you expect to make any money in mail order you must also offer a "full, money-back guarantee if not completely satisfied." If you have a quality product you will get very few returns, but you must promptly return the money if requested.

The mail order business puts you under the same legal obligations as any other business. You must be sure to be absolutely truthful in your advertising or you could be held legally responsible. If you claim your glaze is entirely lead-free, it better be. If you use testimonials in your advertising, they need to be actual testimonials and you need to have permission in writing from the people you are quoting. Just use good common sense and you'll be fine.

☐ PROMOTING YOUR MAIL ORDER BUSINESS

When you advertise in a magazine, newspaper or any other publication, you are promoting your business. All this is great, but there is more that you can do and a lot of it is free. It's called the news release or publicity release. Every new line of crafts you develop is worthy of a news release. Use it to help you build your mail order sales. Often news releases are far more effective than classified ads because by publishing your news release the magazine editor is in fact endorsing your product.

Send your news release to every magazine you feel would be interested in it. Many will publish at least a portion of it and it can be very helpful to your business. I make it a practice to duplicate each news release so that I have sufficient copies to send to all the magazines. I also write a cover letter for each release I send out. It takes time but the results are worth it. It indicates that you have taken a personal interest in their magazine. If I've already advertised in a particular magazine I use the statement; "I've advertised in your magazine with excellent results. Since your readers are interested in what I am doing, I am enclosing a new release that describes . . . ." Be sure you include your name and address , not only for the editors but the readers as well. Also, and this is vital, send a thank-you note to the editor after your news release is published. Such a practice is not only common courtesy but in your best interest because if you establish a good relationship from the beginning, you'll be in a position to get additional publicity when you produce a new design or open a shop, or, or, or.

As the result of a thank-you note that I sent, I was asked if I would permit the magazine to use some of my comments in their advertisements. I promptly gave them permission not only out of common courtesy but I received a bonus because every time they use my comments I receive additional exposure.

Remember that the reason for advertising of any kind is to tell people who might be potential customers about your product. Don't be afraid to try other news outlets. Although most mail order experts avoid advertising in the newspapers you might get some excellent response from a news release sent to a local paper.

□ MARKET COMPATIBILITY

Like any other marketing method discussed, mail order is ideal for some craftsmen and meaningless or repugnant to others. Each craftsman will have to make his own decision based on his research and testing of the various marketing channels available which work and feel comfortable to him or her.

Some types of craft objects seem to sell better via mail order than others. Indeed, there are some that will not sell at all through the mails. I don't care how nice a person you are, they won't sell so don't try. You can develop a successful mail order business only if you play by the rules. Here are the rules as I have learned them.

Your Craft Item(s) Should be Unusual

People expect to find hard-to-find, unusual items in mail order catalogs and magazines. I followed the same research procedure that I suggested you follow earlier in this chapter and looked at the top mail order magazines to discover the items that were available consistently. The most popular items included calligraphy kits, extra wide shoes, chairs that lift to help the elderly arise, energy saving shower heads, wine label albums, dog and cat stain removers, etc., none of which, to sum it up are readily available in stores. If your craft item can be bought at any craft shop, you'd be wise to think twice about mail order.

Your Product Should be Personalized

You may not know it, but the most popular mail order item ever produced are those little personal return address labels that you stick on your envelopes. Other personalized items advertised consistently include: shirts with monograms, brass duplicate paper weights of your business card, pen and ink sketches of your home or church, etc. If our craft product is not currently personalized you might think about how you could personalize it. If you make wooden toys, how about stamping the child's name on each toy. If you make pottery is there a way that you could put a person's name on a mug?

Plan for Repeat Business

No mail order business has ever succeeded with just one product. Why? Because it costs so much to get a buyer much of your profit is eaten up by selling costs. However, once you have an established customer he will keep on buying as long as he is satisfied with your products and service. L.L. Bean in Freeport, Maine is one of the largest mail order companies in the world. Once you order something from them you are put on their mailing list and you receive a new catalog each season. The theory is that once someone has bought they will buy again.

The Product Should be Easily Shipped

Breakable items are difficult to ship and are costly to package properly. The best mail order items are light and unbreakable. Patterns,

designs, cloth items, such as printed fabrics or weavings are all potential winners but pottery — my craft — is abysmal. So direct mail is a
better channel for weavers than for potters.

The Item Should be Easily Reproduced

Mail order has its peaks and valleys. There are times when the
orders pour in and other times when orders are slow. This rule means
that you must be able to gear up or down in response to the demand,
or alternatively to have adequate financing to build your inventory
during slack periods. If you have the good fortune to choose the latter
alternative you will have the business advantage of a constant inventory, enabling you to ship immediately.

Nothing is perfect and nobody expects your mail order business
to meet all of the above criteria but the more of the five characteristics
your craft item(s) do have the better the chances for success in mail
order.

If your mail order campaign is working then you are obviously
meeting your client's needs. But don't stop there! Try other variations,
try sets of items, try different sizes, colors, etc. You might consider
including a questionnaire with your shipment asking customers for their
suggestions. In any event you must plan ahead constantly to bring new
and unusual items to the mail order market. If you find this forward
planning onerous, direct mail or any other variation of mail order marketing is not for you.

□   GETTING OUT

Things do change, and you may find at some time down the
line that you want to get out of the mail order business. Obviously you
must meet your obligations and particularly in mail order, your obligations will continue for a long time as people have a curious way of
holding on to direct mail brochures and magazines for years and then
blithely assume that you still want to sell to them.

So, you will receive orders long after you decide to go out of
business. When you do decide to go out of business you must notify
the post office and change your name and address or terminate the
lease on your post office box. The post office is mandated to deliver all
mail that is deliverable, so simply telling them you are out of business
is not sufficient. You must make it impossible for them to deliver. Then
they will return the letter to the sender.

□   MAIL ORDER MARKETING REVIEW

1. Mail order is one of the fastest growing marketing channels
   because it offers convenience and service.
2. Classified ads are best used to attract interest, to be followed up
   with more detailed information.
3. Two-step ads in classified work better than one-step ads.
4. Direct mail offers the best money making potential in mail
   order.

5. Mail order can make you rich or poor. The odds are in favor of poor.
6. You can get started in the mail order marketing channel for a very small investments.
7. Study successful mail order operations and imitate their marketing plan.
8. Your selling price should be at least six times your product cost.
9. Always key your ads so you can see which advertising is working best in which publication.
10. Keep costs to a minimum; ½¢ per item difference can really add up in mail order.
11. Advertise in proven mail order magazines.
12. Target your ad to your audience.
13. Your ad must excite interest.
14. Test, test, test. . . . .
15. Do your research before you begin any mail order campaign.
16. Use the *Standard Rate and Date Reference* or individual rate cards to determine advertising rates and rules.
17. Start your own in-house advertising agency when your volume warrants it.
18. Use a display ad only after your product has proven profitable through classified ads.
19. Send news releases when you have a new product.
20. Send a thank-you note when a news release is published.
21. Use a list broker to help you decide on the right direct mail list.
22. The hardest part of mail order marketing is waiting for the results to come in.
23. Make sure your craft meets the criteria for successful mail order marketing.
24. Mail order success is based on repeat business.
25. Work to constantly improve your mail order business.
26. Keep your mailing costs to a minimum by mailing in volume.

Chapter 17

Unusual Crafts Outlets

We depart from our usual format here and just jot down a lot of ideas that could mean additional sales to you. The chapter organization in the book is basically the same format I use in my crafts marketing workshops. Some of these marketing ideas are mine, used with great success, others come from workshop participants, and still others come from fellow craftsmen.

☐ THE CONVENTION BUSINESS

Every large city in the United States has a convention bureau. Contact the one nearest you, to get a copy of their projected convention events. The listing will advise who is coming to the city, when, who's in charge, how many people will attend and where the convention will be held. Every convention plans to have a theme or topic related to the host city. In Georgia, typical themes are peaches, dogwoods, and Georgia's red clay.

Give some thought to the characteristics of your area and then make a list of craft items you could make that would be of interest to visitors in your state. Contact the person in charge of the convention and tell him what you do to learn if he would be interested in what you have. He may want to commission you to make individualized gifts for the principal speakers at the convention, or for the officers of the convention. If your media is fabric, perhaps you could print or weave commemorative napkins that the guests take home with them. There are lots of excellent ideas; see what you can come up with.

☐ BANKS

Not too long ago banks never advertised. If you looked carefully you could find them in the yellow pages or the white pages, but that was about the extent of it. Obviously all of this has changed dramatically and presents some opportunities for you as a craftsperson. I know of one weaver who worked out a deal with a bank to allow her to display her work. She agreed to do the installation at no charge, it the bank would supply some administrative help with mailing, printing of invitations, and food and drink for the opening. It all worked out to everyone's satisfaction and she has since done the same thing with several other banks. It gives her exposure and sales (at 100% retail to her) and it gives the banks a good public relations boost.

The bank I deal with has recently instituted an instant 24-hour teller. It is called the Georgia Express and one of their promotional gimmicks was to give train engineer caps to people who signed up for the service. If people opened a new savings account or bought long-term saver certificates, they were given a hand-crafted wooden train done by a local craftsman. Others banks have awarded hand-crafted belt buckles, hand-lettered certificates and other items. Use your imagination to come up with some of your own.

□   CORPORATE SALES

Corporations are always looking for new promotional ideas. The best way to approach them is through their director of public relations. Use the advice call technique to ask for their opinion. You might use the following approach. "Ms. Greensleeves? My name is _____. I am a craftsman working in jewelry. I know that many corporations such as yours often award their employees for outstanding achievements. I'd like to show you my line of hand-crafted jewelry to see if you feel your corporation would be interested. My work can be completely individualized so that you can present a truly personal gift to your employees. Would sometime this week be convenient for you?"

You may not get a sale your first time out, but you'll have made a contact and you may get a call later. It's worth the effort!

□   PROMOTIONAL SALES

Take a few minutes and make a list of people and places that may want some of your craft items to promote something they are doing. If it's a skiing event and you make snowflakes in sterling silver, you have a natural. One craftsperson in my area was commissioned to do stained glass trophies for the winners of the annual road race. How about contacting the local florist to see if she or he would like some hanging planters? If the women's club in your area is sponsoring a fashion show, contact them to see if you might display some of your handwoven items, etc., etc.

I know one craftsperson, a potter, who made arrangements with some real estate agents. She made jars and covered containers out of the local clay. Because the clay was unique to the area, the real estate agents gave one of the hand-thrown clay pieces to people moving into the area as housewarming gifts. It was a super builder of good will!

□ CATALOGS

The granddaddy of the crafts catalogs is the *Goodfellow Catalog of Wonderful Things*, weighing over four pounds, containing 720 pages with 1,500 photos and featuring the works of 680 of America's finest craftspeople. The book (catalog) is designed as a wishbook. People wanting to order any of the crafts do so by contacting the craftsperson directly.

The catalog is now put out in four different editions:

1. *The Goodfellow Catalog of Wonderful Wearables.*
2. *The Goodfellow Catalog of Wonderful Things for Terrific Kids.*
3. *The Goodfellow Catalog of Wonderful Things for In and Around Your Home.*
4. *The Goodfellow catalog of Wonderful Gifts Under $50.00.*

If you are interested in participating your work must first be juried and if accepted there is a $200 fee. The fee is for one of the catalogs only.

The Goodfellow Catalogs, published by Goodfellow Press, Box 4520, Berkeley, CA 94704, have been so successful that other craftspeople and crafts groups are publishing their own catalogs. Check with your state crafts organization for details. One catalog you might want to check out is *The New England Handcraft Catalog*, P.O. Box 459, Nodus, CT, 06469. Another catalog, published by a non-profit crafts group is entitled *Bluebook* and features the work of 66 juried craftspeople. The catalogs are available from the Northwest Crafts Project, 3410 Fremont North, Seattle, WA 98103.

□ CLOTHING STORES

Fine clothing stores and boutiques are looking for crafts to accent their clothing displays. You may not like playing second fiddle but keep in mind that your work is being seen by a clientele that can afford to buy fine clothes — and crafts. Most arrangements are on a consignment basis but you will need to work out the specific details with the store. Take a walk around shopping centers and identify potential markets and then approach the manager. Make sure that you are allowed to display your card so that potential purchasers will know how to get in touch with you.

□ TOURIST CENTERS

Tourist centers forbid commercial displays but many will accept displays of crafts. You'll have better luck here if you are part of a craft organization rather than an individual craftsperson. Get in touch with the Director of Tourism and tell him or her what your group would like to do. It can be excellent advertising for the state and you.

□ AUCTIONS

There are several different approaches here. You might donate your work to a charitable organization to help raise funds. While you don't make any money on this you do get excellent publicity. I believe the best auctions from a promotional standpoint are the educational TV auctions each year. The sponsors are always anxious to receive quality crafts and your work is seen by thousands of people.

Some craftsmen have end-of-the-year auctions at their studios. Others have auctions at other times of the year. Protect yourself by putting minimum bids on your items.

□ RESTAURANTS

There are more and more "theme" restaurants opening up every day. I am not suggesting that you sign a contract with McDonald's or Burger King but there are gourmet restaurants and other speciality restaurants looking for crafts; either to serve on or for decoration. Don't be afraid to contact them and offer your services.

□ WORLD FAIRS

Craftsmen were well represented at the 1982 Knoxville World's Fair. Five craft organizations joined together into a cooperative and sold their work in an arts and crafts gallery. Over 100 artists and craftsmen were participants. In addition crafts groups and individual artists throughout the fair area promoted their crafts to attract the tourist's dollar.

□ MUSEUMS

Not too many years ago museums were pretty stuffy places. If you could buy anything at the museum gift shop it was limited to post cards of the masters, posters, or reproductions, or slides, or museum memberships. Now, however, museums are becoming much more liberal and are showing individual, unique works of individual craftspeople. I believe an advice call to your local museum is the best approach to open up some possible outlets for you.

I predict that some of the outlets listed here as unusual will be typical, profitable outlets for craftsmen in the near future. I even hesitated to place the *Goodfellow Catalogs* in this category because they are already an effective marketing method for many craftspeople. Again, the message is to try it and if it works keep doing it.

PART FIVE

Professional Help

Chapter 18

Keeping the Business

I trust that you have gotten the message by now that selling crafts is a serious business. Craftsmen are known for their independent thinking and free spirit. It is often this desire for personal freedom that attracts people to choosing a career in the crafts. It is also what buyers find attractive about crafts; they symbolize the efforts of an individual spirit.

However, I must caution you not to let that individual spirit be the cause of your failure. I don't care how free-spirited you are, you cannot run your business all by yourself. You need expert help. Business is just too complicated to be able to do it all on your own. If you try you will pay the price, sometimes the loss of your business.

☐ PROFESSIONAL HELP

This section is about where you can get professional help, often free. But before you contact any professional, you must do your homework, and define what it is that you want to do. I'm not talking about a vague statement like "I want to get out of the rat race and make a living making crafts." I'm talking about a detailed, step by step plan for reaching specific goals and that calls for:

☐ LONG RANGE PLANNING

America seems to be a land of instant gratification; instant wealth, fast food, fast cars, casual sex, instant heroes, etc, etc. Craftsmen, although they are more aware than most of how long it takes to produce quality products are still susceptible to the instant success syndrome. Well, life isn't like that. The people who succeed are the people who have a plan and stick with it, adjusting and polishing as they go along.

Allow me to get off the track just a bit here to illustrate the importance of long range planning. I believe that everyone has a desire to be financially independent and there is a way of achieving wealth that works so well that it has been called the "Eighth Wonder of the

World." What is this miracle money maker? It's investing money and letting the principle and interest compound over a period of time. Let me give you an example. If you invested $100 a month in an account paying 12%, starting with your 20th birthday, and did that for 40 years you would have $1,176,477 the day you turned 60. The sad fact is that very few people ever reach this stage. Why? Because they do not have the discipline to plan over a long period of time.

You need to make a plan that will describe where you want to be in one year, two years, five years, ten years and beyond. This plan should include detailed information on what your goals are and how you plan to achieve them. If your goal is to double your sales in five years what plans have you made to accomplish that goal? Does it call for buying equipment that will allow you to increase your volume? Do you plan to hire someone to assist you in the studio?

When you have your plan together it's time to get professional help. Only with it in hand your consultants can be much more valuable because they will be able to help you achieve your goals. This section tells you how to contact experts who can assist you. All of the sources listed can be very valuable but I believe two sources are absolutely essential and they should become part of your long range plan immediately.

Hire a Lawyer

He or she can be invaluable to you. Yes, I know they cost money but if you get a good one they will be worth every penny. Plus you can get more value from your lawyer by preparing several questions or documents to be reviewed at one time. For example, if you are opening a studio, contact all the local agencies, get a copy of the mortgage or lease agreement and any other documents you need and bring them to the lawyer for one session. You'll probably be charged by the hour rather than by the document.

Hire an Accountant

I recommend not just an accountant but a good tax expert. There is a discussion on how a good accountant can help you in the appendix but let me point out here that with your long range business plan in hand an accountant can tailor your buying, selling, depreciation, borrowing and bookkeeping to take advantage of all the tax regulations, saving you hundreds, perhaps thousands of dollars per year.

The crafts business is an exciting, friendly one. There are many fellow craftsmen out there ready and willing to help you. I hope this section helps you locate the ones that you want.

Chapter 19

Do You Need An Agent?

Most craftspeople don't produce the volume to warrant an agent, nor do they sell to a large number of volume outlets. But for some craftspeople an agent can be extremely helpful in marketing work. You should consider the possibility of hiring an agent if:

1. Your production is high and you need to devote more time to it.
2. You have items that can stand a 15% – 25% mark-up at the wholesale level and still be competitively priced at retail. That is two organizations — your agent and the retailer each getting the margins they require.
3. You have high priced items.

The bottom line in considering hiring a sales agent is that it is going to increase the price of your crafts because another person is involved in getting your product to market.

An agent or sales representative makes his money as a percentage of the wholesale selling price for each item he handles. Naturally an agent wants to use his time as effectively as possible so he usually represents several people or manufacturers within a given marketing audience. For example, an agent may represent manufacturers of gift items, or hardware items or garden items or crafts or bath items or, or. . . . Instead of stopping at every shop in town an agent stops at the shops that sell the products he carries, thus using his time more effectively.

Any agent wants to represent a line of products that will sell and give his customers a selection to choose from. However, he does not want to create competition between the people or businesses he represents so he is careful to represent related but non-competitive lines. If you do face mugs and he already represents a potter doing face mugs ethically he should not agree to represent you (or at least your face mugs). some agents represent craftspeople on a limited basis. For example, he may refuse to be your agent for your production work because he already represents a production potter, but he may agree to represent your one-of-a-kind porcelain sculptures. . . .

Unless you have a tremendous personality, own a villa in Spain or have some other unrevealed assets, your agent is not going to represent you for nothing. Most agents work on a commission basis and get paid when you get paid so they have a real interest in your success as a craftsman. The rate of commission varies, ranging from 15% for production type items to 50% of one-of-a-kind high priced items. The commission rate is computed at the wholesale level. Here's how it would work in a typical instance:

CRAFT ITEM: Leather purse

Retail price......................................$60.00
Wholesale price $30.00

Revenue to gallery $30.00
Revenue to agent (15%) ....$ 4.50
Revenue to craftsman.....................$25.50

Can you make a profit? If the figures say you can't you have three choices:

1. Increase your efficiency so you can make each item for less, thus improving your profit margin.
2. Increase your price.
3. Forget about hiring an agent.

It may be of some comfort to know that some agents for fine artists get 50% of the sales price. The arrangement one of my colleagues has is fairly typical. He does large scale sculptural commissions in the $5,000 to $20,000 price range. The arrangement he has with his agent is to deduct his material expenses and overhead expenses from the sales price and divide the remainder, half to himself and half to the agent.

What does an agent do for his fee? Well, essentially he acts as your representative calling on shops, galleries and other outlets to introduce and hopefully sell your work. The big advantage to the craftsperson is that while the agent is engaged in his area of expertise (selling) the craftsperson can engage in his (creating). Thus both parties are making the best use of their respective abilities.

A good agent functions in several other capacities as well. He checks the credit rating of each account, negotiates terms and will report back to you about what people are looking for in your crafts area.

It is your responsibility to furnish your agent with all the sales materials you would want if you were approaching the outlets on your own. These materials might include slides, photos or samples of your work, price lists, order blanks and conditions of sale. Make sure you include in your contract with any agent the commission structure, your credit policy, the term of the contract and how the contract is terminated in the event of default.

□ FINDING THE RIGHT AGENT

This isn't going to be easy because the good ones are already busy and the bad ones won't help you or anyone else. The best way is by word of mouth. Talk to fellow craftspeople and see if they have an agent or know who does. If they are satisfied with their agent's service, call him and make an appointment to show your work. You may be told in the beginning that he is not accepting any more clients. If that is the case ask if he can recommend someone else who might be willing to represent you. He probably knows of one or two agents.

Some craft agents advertise their services in crafts publications such as *American Crafts* and *The Crafts Report*. You may want to contact one or two to see if there is a good fit. Keep in mind that you are looking for an agent who will help you. Ask for references and ask him what his sales record is. This is a negotiating process, and if it is not an arrangement that will be mutually beneficial then there is no need to work together.

When you do find an agent, he will look at your work and decide if it's saleable. Remember that he knows from experience what sells at the businesses *he* calls on and what doesn't. When an agent does agree to represent you (and you agree to be represented by him) his first question will be whether you can keep him supplied. The agent makes his living selling and if he has nothing to sell he will not make money. If he sells 300 of your $10 (wholesale) items, his commission is $450, but if you only produce and deliver 30 items, his commission becomes $45. He won't stick with you long if you cannot fill the orders that he produces for you.

On the other side of the coin, a good agent should be able to sell all you produce. If he cannot then you have the right to look elsewhere. Make sure that you understand the conditions of the agreement you sign with the agent so that you know who can terminate the contract and under what circumstances.

Most agents want an exclusive for their geographical area. That means that you may want to work with several agents, each representing you in a particular geographical area. Do not, under any circumstances, try to go out and do your own selling in any agent's territory. He'll lose his commission and his temper.

It is a good idea to specify the length of time that an agent will have an exclusive right to sell your crafts. After all, if he is not selling you want to get someone else. If the agent does do a good job of selling your wares he will want to sign a contract for a longer period of time but it is wise in the beginning to specify how long the agent will have to prove himself. It's a little like signing a sales agreement with a real estate agent to sell your house. Six to twelve months is a normal period of which to grant an exclusive agreement. If the crafts are not sold, you and the agent will want to terminate the contract. A sample contract is shown in Appendix D.

□   YOUR AGENT DOESN'T ONLY SELL

Your agent is an extremely valuable resource person. He can help you in two ways; by keeping you informed of what the market is like in his territory and by representing you to customers who otherwise would never come in contact with your work.

Let your agent know that you welcome his advice and observations. Ask him if he's seen anything in his travels that would complement what you are already producing.

Keep your agent informed of any changes or modifications you are making in your line. He may have some suggestions for you, but most importantly he will need to know what you are doing so that he can accurately represent you to his customers.

Chapter 20

What to do if Your Work Isn't Selling

Nobody, not even the highest paid marketing experts, can tell you what will sell and what won't. Marketing experts earn their money because they know how to find out what will sell by testing, testing, testing. You need to be your own expert and test each one of your craft items in the marketplace.

Poor sales happen to all of us, even when we are convinced we have a sure winner on our hands. There have been times when I would have staked my reputation on a particular item being a best seller but it flopped miserably. A small modification in an item selling poorly can increase sales dramatically.

The people in my crafts marketing workshops frequently come afterwards to say, "You know, it's encouraging to know that other people make mistakes too!" Nobody is successful every time. Remember that most new products never make it to the marketplace so why should you expect everything that you do to be successful. When things don't work out there are two things you can do:

1. Feel sorry for yourself and give up.
2. Find out why things didn't work and change it so it will work.

Let me give you an example. I started my pottery business making a series of birds. I had gotten the idea from a potter in England while on a teacher exchange program. Nobody was using this particular technique in the United States so my birds were unique. I was sure that they would sell well and this time I was right.

I took samples to several shops in my area and quickly learned that I had success on my hands. Dreams of the big time became more and more real, but I got tired of signing all the little birds, so I started stamping them. I wanted to sound professional, so I stamped each bird with the name I had decided upon for my "big time" pottery: The Exeter Pottery Works. For a few dollars, the local print shop made a rubber stamp for me and I was in business.

I started making birds and stamping them like crazy. The shops and galleries all wanted more, so off I went with my newly made, newly stamped birds. Because the first orders of birds sold so well, the shops increased their orders, and I began producing them by the hundreds. After the stamped birds were all delivered, I started in again, anticipating not only additional orders from my regular outlets but also from new shops and galleries. I made birds for a month but noticed that they were beginning to pile up. Two more weeks passed before I called a few galleries to see what was happening. Nobody had an answer, they all said the birds were attracting a lot of interest but people simply were not buying.

The next Saturday, I went to one of the galleries that had sold a large number and hung around (with the owner's permission) to watch the customers. My birds were well displayed, people picked them up and looked at them, looked at the bottom and put them down again. I should have caught on then, but didn't. Finally, I walked up to a lady who had picked up several birds only to put them down. I said, "Excuse me. I notice you have been looking at those birds. I'm interested in them myself. Do you know who the artist is?" She said, "Oh, you don't want those! I liked them too, but they're not done by an artist. They're done by a commercial company. See! Here on the bottom, Exeter Potter Works." I had my answer!

I went home, threw out all the stamped birds, made new ones, signed each one and took them to the shops to replace the stamped ones. It was an expensive lesson and it has taken a little time to tell, but it contains an important message for every craftsperson. People buy what appeals to them and they generally buy crafts because they are unique, personal and hand-made. Anything you do to convey that message will help sales!

A couple of other quick personal examples might help. I made porcelain mirrors with a variety of cobalt blue designs on them. They were well crafted, priced competitively and were admired by many people, but weren't selling. Why? The hanger I had on the back did not look strong enough. People were afraid that they they would drop and break. A sturdier hanger resulted in increased sales. In another instance, my spoon jars were not selling well because they were too short. I made longer ones and sales increased.

Talk to any craftsperson and they can cite their own examples, but there is always a reason and nine times out of ten it is a very simple one — all you have to do is find out what it is. I recommend that you begin your investigation by seeking the answers to three questions about your product:

1. Do you have it in the right place?
2. Are you selling at the right price?
3. Do your customers know about your product?

Market

The whole purpose of this book is to assist you in finding the right market for your craft. Something that will sell well at craft shows will not sell in mail-order and something that sells well in galleries will most likely be a disaster at a mall show. So the first thing you do is to check to see if you are marketing your product in the right marketing channel. If you are the only craftsman selling hand-made leather belts through mail-order it's possible you have chosen the wrong marketing channel.

Within each marketing channel there is tremendous variability as well. There are over 50 galleries in my geographical area, each appealing to a different clientele. The people who buy mail-order items through *Popular Science* are not at all like the people who respond to mail-order ads in *Gourmet*. Every mall show and craft fair is different as well, particularly established shows. People grow to expect a certain type of craft and go back year after year in search of it. People go to prestige shows expecting to get top quality crafts at top prices while most mall shows attract buyers who respond to impulse buying and low priced items.

Price

Just as different markets attract different buyers, they attract people willing to pay certain prices. If your product is in the same price range as numerous other items in the same market channel you should be all right, but it's possible to be underpriced or overpriced. If your item is significantly lower priced than most of the other items some buyers will get the impression that your work is of inferior quality. If, on the other hand, your work is priced significantly higher than all the others, some buyers will wonder who the hell you think you are charging that much for one of your pieces.

Product Knowledge

The more people know about your product the more they will pay for it. Remember that buyers perceive things according to their standards, not yours.

I know one potter whose sales were poor in one particular shop. Investigation indicated that his problem had to do with product knowledge. He specialized in crystal glazes, a highly technical, difficult, time consuming process. His were the only ceramics in the shop using such costly glazes. Naturally he needed to charge more for his work because of the time and expense involved. The problem was that the buying public did not know what was involved and what made his ceramic pieces unique and so costly. He rectified the problem by attaching an explanatory card to each piece and placing his work in galleries that featured work in the same price range as his.

I've covered the major categories to check, but here are some other things worth looking into:

Color: Some colors sell well in one location and not in another. Keep track of your sales and see what colors sell best in each market channel.

Size: People are trained to expect to pay more for large items than small items. There is an unwritten law in crafts that says that certain things of a certain size should be a certain price. Often you can increase sales simply by making your object a little larger and charging the same price.

Finish: Don't overlook this one! People are very, very careful about buying crafts and they look at them from every angle before they buy. Don't leave any rough edges, seams, spots, stains, or blemishes of any kind.

Selection: Do whatever you can to assure that the customer has a selection to choose from, whether you are selling your work through a gallery, at a crafts fair, or any other marketing channel. Would you buy a new car from a dealer who only had one car to choose from? Buyers like to choose what they want.

Style: People buy crafts for many reasons but one of the most important is that they know they were made by a real live human being. They like to know that you are serious about what you do and that you are an expert which in turn means having a style. Naturally you'll need to experiment as you are developing your style but as soon as possible you need to develop a consistent range of items that people can rely on and can count on getting when they want them.

☐   WHAT DO PEOPLE REALLY THINK OF YOUR WORK?

This can be a frightening question at first. But knowing what your customers really think of your work is essential; often making the difference between your success or failure. There are two sources of valuable information, the owners of galleries, shops and wholesale buyers to whom you sell your work and the customers who buy directly from you. Let them know that you welcome honest, objective comments about your work. Their comments can point out things you never thought about but may be a major reason for your poor sales.

It's easy to ask gallery owners about your work and they will respect you for it. Remember that the better your work sells at their gallery, the more money they make, so naturally they have an interest in helping you make your work more appealing. It's a little more difficult getting feed-back from customers who buy directly from you, but here's one way. Whenever you sell something directly to a customer, whether it's from your studio or at a crafts fair, see if you can get the customer's name and address and phone number. In a few weeks call the customer to learn if he is enjoying his purchase. It builds good will, gives you very important feed-back about your product and often generates additional sales.

☐ MILLION DOLLAR INFORMATION FOR FREE

Large corporations spend millions of dollars each year to survey their customers. The reason they are willing to invest such sums of money is simple. The more they can find out about what the customer wants the more closely they can match their product to the customer's wants and the more they sell. You can do the same kind of customer survey for little or no money, just an investment of time and effort. Remember there is always a reason your product isn't selling, and the quicker you find out the faster you can modify it or your marketing strategy so that you profit from your efforts.

Chapter 21

Copyrighting Your Work

Copyright laws exist for your protection, but you have to know what they will and will not do. In addition, you should be aware of when it's advisable to copyright and when it's not.

First, there seems to be some confusion about copyright and patent. A patent is granted by the government as a guarantee that the inventor of a new or unusual product or process will have exclusive rights to the production, use and sale of his work for a specific time, usually seventeen years. Patent applications must be accompanied by drawings or diagrams, along with a sworn oath signed by the applicant that he believes himself to be the original inventor.

A filing fee (usually around $65) must be paid for each application. When a patent is approved, the specifications are printed in the Patent Office Register and made available to the public. Interested parties may use the diagrams to assist them in the development of their own designs or after the patent expires, to produce the invention or process themselves. There are now over 3,000,000 patents on file, all of which are available to the public.

A copyright, on the other hand, gives the creator an exclusive right to make and sell copies of original works. Additionally, the exclusive right is granted for a much longer period of time than is granted for patents.

☐   WHAT CAN BE COPYRIGHT?

Just about anything of a creative nature can be copyright. These include such things as plays, musicals, dances, motion pictures, sound recordings, as well as pictorial, graphic and sculptural works. A copyright may be claimed for any original work that exhibits some intellectual effort on the creator's part. Originality is understood to mean a work that has not been copied from another source, but is the result of independent effort by the creator. You'll be interested to know that originality is not determined by novelty, ingenuity or aesthetic merit. How originality is determined is open to some debate.

Production craft items are usually classified as applied art. This classification covers works primarily designed to serve a utilitarian purpose. However the copyright only protects that element of the utilitarian object that is uniquely designed. As a potter you would be able to copyright the unique design you used to decorate the plate, but not the plate itself. If you are a weaver you would be able to copyright a design that you used on a place mat but not the place mat itself.

One-of-a-kind crafts would come under the pictorial graphic and sculptural works category, for which the entire article can be copyright.

□   THE LEGAL BASIS FOR COPYRIGHT

As of January 1, 1978, all works which can be copyright are governed by the Copyright Act of 1976. The Copyright Act of 1976 grants the owner of the copyright the exclusive right to do any of the following:

1. Reproduce the work.
2. Prepare and produce derivative works. Thus, if you designed a doll that was extremely successful you might want to produce brothers, sisters, animals etc., etc. for the original doll. These spin-offs are derivative works.
3. Distribute copies or recordings of the copyrighted work to the public.
4. Display the copyrighted work publicly.

Ownership

Ownership of copyright work belongs to the craftsman unless it is transferred to another party attested by a written document. However, there are two exceptions. If the creator is an employee and the work is created during normal business hours, the employer is considered the copyright holder. This means that should your assistant or apprentice create something while working for you, you are the holder of the copyright, should one be sought.

The other exception occurs when you specifically contract something out to someone else to perform for you. Let's suppose that you make dolls and that you make everything but the dresses. If you contract with your neighbor down the street to make the dresses specifically for your dolls you would be considered the holder of the copyright.

Transfer of Copyright

The creator of any craft object may transfer his exclusive copyright to another party or it may be bequeathed by will. If you designed a fabric, you could license a company to reproduce and distribute your work for a fee but still retain the copyright including the right to create the derivative designs. Any transfer of copyright must be in writing and must be signed by the copyright owner. As the copyright owner you may terminate the copyright license agreement at any time unless the contract specifies something to the contrary. In other words, if you agree to license the ABC Company to reproduce and sell the work you can withdraw from that agreement at any time. The withdrawal agreement was included in the 1976 Copyright Act to prevent unprofitable or undesirable licensing. If the ABC Company falsely represents itself and started producing an inferior reproduction of your original design you could stop them by withdrawing your license agreement.

□ LENGTH OF COPYRIGHT

Any creative work you copyright continues in its copyright from the day of its creation for the life of the creator, plus fifty years. If the work is created by two people the copyright is valid for the life of the last surviving creator, plus fifty years.

□ SALE OF OBJECT

The sale of a copyrighted object, whether it is a painting, a pot, a weaving or any other creative product does not give the owner right to copyright ownership. In other words, Shady Simon Legree, the potter down the street, cannot buy one of your pots, display the sales slip, and make 1,000 copies of the same pot to sell at his own studio, or at the next craft show.

□ NOTICE OF COPYRIGHT

Undistributed works do not have to be copyrighted but as soon as you start making copies and selling them they should be copyrighted. The regulations say that the copyright notice must be firmly attached and that it be clearly visible. A copyright statement on a card attached to a stoneware mug would be clearly visible but would not be considered firmly attached. Crafts made of clay, wood, metal, plastic or other similar materials should have the copyright stamped directly into or onto the surface. Crafts made from fabrics should have the copyright notice printed on a label that is sewn securely to the original fabric.

The copyright notice should be placed on the original work and the copies of that work prior to public distribution. Note that the copyright can be lost if suitable notice is not placed on every item. However, if you do forget initially, you can, by showing a reasonable effort to label the items you initially missed, still retain ownership. You can take such action within five years of the original distribution of the product and still retain your copyright. The copyright notice you attach to your craft must have three elements:

1. The copyright designation, 'copyright', the abbreviation 'copr.' or the encircled ©.
2. The name of the copyright owner or a recognizable abbreviation, i.e., B.T. Jefferson.
3. The year of the original design of the work.

Therefore, a suitable copyright notice on one of my craft objects would read:

Copyright
B.T. Jefferson
1983

☐ HOW TO OBTAIN A COPYRIGHT

Write to the United States Copyright Office; Library of Congress; Washingtion, D.C. 20540, tell them you are a craftsman and want to copyright your work. The appropriate forms will be returned in the mail. Complete the form and send back, along with a $10 filing fee. In due time the Copyright Office will return one copy of the form you filed, confirming the date your copyright was registered. Keep in mind that a claim copyright does not guarantee protection but you cannot claim infringement of your copyright unless a copyright has been registered. You must register each individual item; a single copyright cannot cover a series, a collection or any other group of works of art.

The U.S. Copyright Office has a 24-hour information number. Call them direct at 202-987-9100 and ask for form VA.

☐ COPYRIGHT VIOLATION

Suppose you copyright a design for a wooden toy in the form of a duck, put some wheels on it and make some wings out of leather. You take 100 of them to a mall show only to discover that a toymaker 27 booths down the mall has the same duck toy. What can you do to claim violation of your copyright? After checking that *your* duck is copyright and that eack duck is clearly labeled with *your* copyright you have to prove that:
1. The other craftsperson had previous access to your design. In other words, you must prove that somehow the other craftsman saw your ducks and then copied the design. This is a crucial point because if you cannot show evidence of infringement the other craftsman can claim (perhaps rightfully so) that his design is the product of his own imagination and that any similarity is entirely coincidental.
2. The works (yours and the claimed copy) are substantially similar when viewed by the public. In the eyes of the law the two ducks have to look like they were made by the same craftsman or studio. Just because you make ducks and another craftsman makes ducks, you cannot claim copyright infringement.

☐ WHAT SHOULD YOU COPYRIGHT?

There is no need to copyright everything that you make. If you are a potter and make mugs, honey jars, garlic keepers and other production items, you would not want or need copyright. However, if you design an original ceramic piece that is being made nowhere else and can be easily reproduced I'd certainly copyright it. It makes no difference whether the work costs $10,000 or $10, the copyright protects the originality of the design.

One of the principal factors in deciding to copyright is whether the work is easily reproducible. The classic example is the artist Robert Indiana who originated the famous LOVE painting. A short time after the work was displayed, the design was produced on posters, t-shirts, napkins, etc., etc. Indiana's fame but not his fortune increased because he failed to copyright the work. If you do a commission for a particular group or individual, and it's one-of-a-kind, you need not copyright it. If, on the other hand, you design a belt buckle that can be easily mass-produced, a copyright would be in order.

□   PROTECTING YOUR COPYRIGHT

Anyone filing for copyright does so to protect his property rights. If someone infringes upon your rights it is your responsibility to defend your property rights by suing the copier. Copyright laws are open to some interpretation, so unless the infringement is so blatant that anyone can clearly see that the copy is an exact duplicate of your original work I recommend that you engage an attorney skillful in copyright law. After all, someone is taking away your dearest possession, your uniqueness.

APPENDICES

Appendix A

Helpful Agencies, People

Your plan to make a living doing what you enjoy doing as an independent businessman is a common desire. Others may not want to make their living as a craftsman, but they seek the same independence you do. Fortunately there are people and organizations having the interest and experience to help everyone seeking independence.

☐ THE SMALL BUSINESS ADMINISTRATION

One of the best investments the United States Government has ever made was in the Small Business Administration. The S.B.A. was established in 1953 to promote and support small business. It has been doing that professionally ever since. Research indicates that over 90% of all businesses in the United States come under the heading of small business so the need for the services of the S.B.A. is obvious. There are numerous services available through the S.B.A. These services range from publications to in-house consultancy.

There are hundreds of books and publications available from the S.B.A. at little or no cost. They cover every business topic imaginable — advertising, cost control, bookkeeping, borrowing money, taxes, etc. Contact the S.B.A. branch nearest you and ask for their list of publications. The list is free. Some of the information deals with specific problems that a craftsperson may encounter. Other publications are of a more general nature, but I've found all of their material to be helpful.

☐ WORKSHOPS AND SEMINARS

If you live near an S.B.A. center or don't mind traveling a bit, you can benefit from their excellent workshops and seminars. The topics cover an impressive range of business issues and are offered at minimal cost. I've attended several and found every one to be worthwhile. The people conducting the workshops are well-informed and happy to respond to your specific questions.

I've also learned a lot from other people attending the workshop. After all, they are interested in the same thing I am; financial independence through owning and operating my own business.

Information about the schedule and location of the S.B.A. workshops and seminars is available through the local S.B.A. office. Announcements are also published in local papers and sometimes in regional magazines. I still feel the best bet is to contact your state S.B.A. for information because many of the workshops are conducted in series and you may want to plan to attend only the ones that interest you.

□ INDIVIDUAL COUNSELING SERVICES

I like to think that the older I get, the more intelligent I become. Whether or not that is true may be debated, but let's at least assume that experience is a good teacher. The S.B.A. has organized a group of highly experienced, highly trained individuals who offer you personal counseling on your specific business problem through their Service Core of Retired Executives (SCORE).

Members of SCORE volunteer their time to counsel people starting or running their own small business. These volunteers know their stuff and can really help you out, if you contact them in time.

Statistics show that nine out of ten business failures are due to mismanagement. The sad part is that many of these failed businesses could have been saved if they had received expert advice in time. The range of expert experience available through SCORE is impressive and includes doctors, lawyers, accountants, bankers, foreign trade specialists, electronics and computer wizards, advertising and public relations executives and many, many more. Craftspeople have a particular advantage when working with SCORE volunteers because a high percentage of the volunteers are interested in crafts, either because they once thought of becoming a craftsperson or because a craft has become a hobby in retirement.

Another counseling group affiliated with the S.B.A. is the Active Corp of Executives (ACE). This group is similar to SCORE, but is staffed by active executives who have volunteered a portion of their time to assist people like yourself. The services of ACE or SCORE are free. When you invite one to your studio, all their expenses (travels, meals, etc.) are paid by the S.B.A.

Should you decide to enlist the services of an ACE or SCORE volunteer, all you need do is contact the S.B.A. office nearest you. It is important to remember, however, that you should contact these volunteers to help you with a specific problem. Don't call the S.B.A. and say, "I need to talk to any ACE or SCORE volunteer right away! I'm thinking about starting a crafts business and want to know how to do it." Remember, these volunteers are highly trained, highly experienced professionals in their particular fields. Take advantage of their expertise by calling the S.B.A. saying, "I run a small crafts business and am developing an advertising campaign to expose my business to a larger audience. I have some ideas, but would like some advice as to how to go about it. Can you suggest someone who could help?" Another appropriate request would be: "My bookkeeping system is taking up too much of my time, and I don't think it's all that accurate. Do you have anyone in your program who could show me how to set up a simple, efficient, bookkeeping system?" Your request will be honored quickly, efficiently and at no cost to you. Where else can you get a better deal?

☐ FINANCIAL HELP FROM THE S.B.A.

The S.B.A. offers a wide range of services designed to help you finance your small business. Basically, the S.B.A. is a guarantor of funds and works through local banks.

Here's how it works. You've done your homework and have figured that it will cost you $15,000 to get the gallery established. You have $5,000 in your savings account, so you will need to borrow $10,000 in order to get your dream gallery going.

You contact your local banker and submit an application for a small business loan in the amount of $10,000. A few days later, you are informed that your loan wasn't approved.

Now is the time to contact the S.B.A. In fact, S.B.A. will not look at a loan application unless it has been turned down by a bank or two. When you apply for a loan to the S.B.A. you're not really applying for a loan. You're applying for a loan guarantee. If the S.B.A. acts favorably on your loan, they will send you back to the bank that just turned you down. Only this time you are in a much better position because you can take with you a document from the S.B.A. that says that the S.B.A., as an official agency of the government guarantees repayment of your loan, should you be unable to pay it back yourself. The bank is now assured that it will get back what it loans you plus interest. No bank will refuse a loan like that!

The S.B.A. will also issue direct loans under some circumstances, but it is rarely done. Check *directly* with your S.B.A. office for complete details.

☐ THE VOLUNTEER LAWYERS FOR THE ARTS

A friendly free lawyer is just around the corner! There are certain restrictions, but they are minimal, and if you do qualify you can get all sorts of free legal advice on such topics as taxes, copyright, licenses, incorporating etc., etc. Each state has its own V.L.A. office. They can be located in the telephone directory of each state capitol.

In addition to offering free legal advice to the individual craftsperson, the V.L.A. also publishes some excellent booklets and manuals. Here are the ones that I think to be the most worthwhile.
1. *An Introduction to Contracts for The Visual Artist.* San Francisco Bay Area Lawyers for The Arts, 1980, 34 p., $3.50.
2. *An Artist's Handbook on Copyright* (with appendices) Georgia Volunteer Lawyers for The Arts, Inc. 1981, $6.95.
3. *Basic Law for the Artist.* San Francisco Bay Area Lawyers for The Arts. $2.00.

4. *Law and The Arts, Arts and The Law.* Lawyers for The Creative Arts/Chicago. 1979, $6.95.

You probably have a personal lawyer. But you may find that a V.L.A., expert in the art area, is more helpful in craft related problems. The V.L.A. office in your state should be able to refer you to a lawyer in your area who is familiar with the issues you face. If not, all is not lost.

Check with local craftspeople to learn who they consult for their legal problems. Obviously some craftspeople will have a lawyer and others won't, so if you run into a blank wall here you need to consult your local crafts organization. They will have names of lawyers who have either volunteered to help craftspeople or who will charge a fee but are well acquainted with the arts.

□ ACCOUNTANTS

Here again, a good accountant is a good accountant who has experience working with artists and craftspeople can be a great accountant. Why? Because contrary to popular belief accounting is not an exact science. There are many issues open to interpretation and how your finances are interpreted can mean a big difference in your profit-and-loss column and the amount of tax you pay or don't pay each year.

Allow me to cite just one example where familiarity with the arts can help your accountant save you money: Depreciation. Every single piece of equipment in your studio has its own depreciation schedule. The IRS has established guidelines for depreciation schedule. The IRS has established guidelines for depreciation of standard tools and equipment such as typewriters, copiers, etc. But there are no standard schedules for looms, kilns, foundries, chisels, etc. An accountant, familiar with the arts has acquired through experience a knowledge of the average rate of depreciation on a whole range of arts and craft tools. More importantly he can defend these rates in an IRS audit if needed.

There are many other instances where an art-knowledgeable accountant can help. Let's face it, craftspeople are not always the most organized people in the world and a sympathetic accountant can do wonders to sort out the mess. Let me share something with you that my accountant shared with me. He worked for years in the IRS and knows what he's talking about. (In my opinion, anyway.)

1. The IRS is much less likely to audit a return that has been professionally prepared because they know from experience that often the preparers know more about taxes and IRS regulations than the IRS does.

2. Almost all returns are scanned by computer. There are certain "keys" that the computer looks for. If one or more "keys" are found, the computer signals the return for audit. A good accountant will keep "keys" out of your return.

It is not my intent to suggest that you defraud the government. I am pointing out that you are entitled to every legal deduction and when you own your own business the complexities of the tax laws can be confusing. Find a good accountant by asking fellow craftspeople who they use to prepare their returns and go to for financial advice.

□ FELLOW CRAFTSPEOPLE

You may want to contact these people individually or through an organization. Regardless, I have found with few exceptions, very few exceptions, that craftspeople are a very congenial group and really enjoy helping one another. Don't be afraid to contact them.

Appendix B

Craft Associations and Organizations

Space limitations prevent me from listing local craft associations. Your state arts agency can easily supply you with a list of the craft groups in your state. Most of the organizations listed in this section are special interest groups, i.e., The California Carver's Guild or Crochet Association International.

The two associations that serve craftspeople regardless of their chosen studio field are: The American Crafts Council and the World Crafts Council.

American Crafts Council; 22 W. 55th Street; New York, NY 10019; phone: 212/397-0600. Founded: 1943; members: 35,000. Publish *American Craft*, bimonthly.

California Carver's Guild; P.O. Box 1195; Cambria, CA 93428; phone: 408/245-1858. Founded: 1974; members: 1700. President: Allan Fougner. Publish *The Log*, monthly.

Center for the History of American Needlework; Old Economy Village; 14th and Church Streets; Ambridge, PA 15003; phone: 414/266-6440. Founded: 1974; members: 500. Executive Director: Rachel Maines. Publish *Counted Thread*, quarterly.

Counted Thread Society of America; 3305 S. Newport Street; Denver, CO 80224; phone: 303/758-6637. Editor: Elizabeth Stears. Founded: 1974; subscribers: 14,000. Publish *Counted Thread*, quarterly.

Crochet Association International; P.O. Box 131; Dalles, GA 30132; phone: 404/445-7137. Executive Director: William E. Elmore. Founded: 1976; members: 15,000. Publish 27 crochet instruction booklets.

Embroiderer's Guild of America; Six E. 45th Street; Room 1501; New York, NY 10017; phone: 212/986-0460. Founded: 1950; members: 23,500. Publish *Needle Arts*, quarterly.

Handweavers Guild of America; 65 LaSalle Road; West Hartford, CT 06107; phone: 203/233-5124. President: Roger A. Thomason. Founded: 1969; members: 20,075. Publish *Shuttle Spindle & Dyepot.*

International Guild of Craft Journalists, Authors and Photographers; 3632 Ashworth, N.; Seattle, WA 98103; phone: 206/632-7222. Founded: 1976; members: 265. President: Michael Scott. Publish *Guild Bulletin quarterly.*

International Old Lacers; P.O. Box 1029; Westminster, CO 80030. Founded: 1953; members: 2200. President: Vada Belle Bledsoe. Publish *Bulletin,* bimonthly; *Members Directory,* annually.

International Porcelain Artist Teachers; 4125 N.W. 57th; Oklahoma City, OK 73112; phone: 405/946-7121. Executive Secretary: Mary Nokes. Founded: 1956; members: 3000. Publish *Newsletter.*

Marquetry Society of America; 32-24 53rd Street; Flushing, NY 11354; phone: 212/463-8749. Trustee: Allan E. Fitchett. Founded: 1972; members: 1500. Publish *Newsletter,* 10 issues per year.

National Association for Safety and Health in the Arts and Crafts; Five Beekman Street; New York, NY 10038; phone: 212/227-6220. Executive Director: Michael McCann. Publish *Arts Hazards Newsletter,* 10 issues per year.

National Guild of Decoupeurs; 807 Rivard Boulevard; Grosse Pointe, MI 48230; phone: 313/882-0682. Executive Director: Ann Standish. Founded: 1971; members; 500. Publish *Decoupage Dialogue,* monthly.

National Quilting Association; Box 62; Greenbelt, MD 20770; phone: 301/474-5319. President: Alice V. Skarda. Founded: 1970; members: 3500. Publish *Patchwork Patter.*

National Society of Tole and Decorative Painters; P.O. Box 808; Newton, KS 67114; phone: 316/283-9665. Executive Director: Margy Wentz. Founded: 1972; members: 16,000. Publish *The Decorative Painter,* 6 issues per year.

National Woodcarver's Association; 7424 Miami Avenue; Cincinnati, OH 45243; phone: 513/561-9051. President: Ed F. Gallenstein. Founded: 1953; members: 16,000. Publish *Chip Chats,* bimonthly.

Smocking Arts Guild of America; P.O. Box 75; Knoxville, TN 37901; phone: 615/637-5456. Executive Director: Carol S. Wigginton. Founded: 1979; members: 1370.

Society of American Goldsmiths; 8589 Wonderland, N.W.; Clinton, OH 44216; phone: 216/854-2681. President: Thomas R. Markusen. Founded: 1970; members: 2500. Publish *Metalsmith Magazine*, quarterly.

Society of Crafts Designers; P.O. Box 2176; Newburgh, NY 12550; phone: 914/565-3118. Executive Director: Ruth P. Linesey. Founded: 1975; members: 185. Publish *Newsletter*, bimonthly.

World Crafts Council; 22 W. 55th Street; New York, NY 10019; phone: 212/265-5840. Founded: 1964; members: 84 countries.

Appendix C

Craft Books
and Magazines

□ BOOKS

My apologies to authors of books not listed here. There are hundreds of excellent crafts books available on every conceivable topic. The books listed here deal with craft marketing issues, such as the pamphlets published by the American Crafts Council on packing and shipping crafts and photographing crafts.

American Crafts Council; 22 W. 55th Street; New York, NY 10019

Packing and Shipping Crafts. 1977.

Photographing Crafts. 1974.

American Crafts Council. *Pricing and Promotion: A Guide for Craftspeople.* McGuire, Patrick and Moran, Lois, eds., 1979.

Arnold, Arnold. *The Complete Book of Arts and Crafts: An Encyclopedic Sourcebook of Techniques, Tools, Ideas and Instruction.* N.A.L., 1977.

Becker, Louis. *How to Make and Sell Your Arts and Crafts.* Fell, 1975.

Brabec, Barbara. *Creative Cash: How to Sell Your Crafts, Needlework, Designs and Know-How.* H.P. Books, 1981.

Carravor, Natalie. *Sell Your Photographs: The Complete Marketing Strategy for the Freelancer.* Madrona Publications, 1979.

Chamberlain, Betty. *The Artist's Guide to His Market.* Watson-Guptill, 1979.

Chicorel, Marietta, ed. *Chicorel Index to the Crafts: Ceramics, Leather and Wood.* Vol. 13B. American Library Publishing company, 1977.

Chicorel, Marietta, ed. *Chicorel Index to the Crafts: Glass, Enamel, Metal.* Vol. 13A American Library Publishing Company, 1977.

Chicorel, Marietta, ed. *Chicorel Index to the Crafts: Needlework, Crochet to Tie Dye.* Vol. 13. American Library Publishing company, 1977.

Cochrane, Diane. *This Business of Art.* Watson-Guptill, 1978.

Davis, Sally A., ed. *Artist's Market.* Writer's Digest, 1982.

Eaton, Allen H. *Handicrafts of the Southern Highlands.* Peter Smith.

Genfan, Herb and Taetzsch, Lyn. *How to Start Your Own Crafts Business.* Watson-Guptill, 1974.

Glassman, Judith. *National Guide to Craft Supplies.* Van Nostrand Reinhold, 1975.

Goodman, Calvin J. *Art Marketing Handbook.* Gee Tee Bee, 1978.

Katchen, Carole. *Promoting and Selling Your Art!* Watson-Guptill, 1978.

Lewis, Ralph. *Making and Managing an Art and Craft Shop.* David and Charles, 1971.

Paz, Octabio and World Crafts Council. *In Praise of Hand: Contemporary Crafts of the World.* New York Graphic Society, 1974.

Scott, Michael. *The Crafts Business Encyclopedia: Marketing, Management and Money.* Harcourt, Brace, Jovanovich, 1979.

Smith, Sharon, ed. *Handcraft Centers of New England.* Yankee Books, 1981.

Sommer, Elyse. *Career Opportunities in Crafts: The First Complete Guide for Success as a Crafts Professional.* Crown, 1977.

Torbet, Laura. *The Scribner Encyclopedia of Crafts.* Three volumes. Scribner, 1980.

To Survey American Crafts: A Planning Study (National Endowment for the Arts Research Division Reports). Number 2, Publishing Center for Cultural Resources, 1980.

Wigginton, Eliot. *Foxfire Books,* editions 1 — 5. Doubleday, 1972 — present.

□ MAGAZINES

Here are some magazines that will be helpful in marketing and promoting your work. Some magazines are listed in this section and again in the section on associations as many associations publish magazines for their membership.

American Artist Business Letter; 1515 Broadway; New York, NY 10036 (10 issues per year).

American Craft; 22 W. 55th Street; New York, NY 10019 (membership American Crafts Council; bimonthly).

Art and the Law; Volunteer Lawyers for the Arts; 36 W. 44th Street; New York, NY 10036 (8 issues per year).

Canada Crafts; Nonis Publications; 2453 Vonge Street; Suite 102; Toronto, Ontario M4P 2E8 (bimonthly).

Ceramics Monthly; Circulation Department; Box 12448; Columbus, OH 43212 (monthly except July and August).

Ceramics Review; 172 Newbury Street; London, England WIV 1LE (bimonthly).

Crafts; P.J.S. Publications, Inc.; News Plaza; Box 1790; Peoria, IL 61656 (monthly).

Crafts; Crafts Council; 12 Waterloo Place; London, England SW1Y 4AV (bimonthly).

Craftsnews; Ontario Crafts Council; 346 Dundas Street; W. Toronto, Ontario M5T 165 Canada (membership Ontario Crafts Council; 8 issues per year).

Crafts 'N Things; Clapper Publishing Co., Inc.; 14 Main Street; Park Ridge, IL 60068 (bimonthly).

Creative Crafts; Carstens Publishing, Inc.; Box 700; Newton, NJ 07860 (6 issues per year).

Decorating & Craft Ideas; Tandy Corporation; Box C-30; Birmingham, AL 35201 (monthly).

The Crafts Report; 700 Orange Street; P.O. Box 1992; Wilmington, DE 19899.

Fiberarts; 50 College Street; Asheville, NC 28801 (bimonthly).

Fine Woodworking; Subscription Department; Taunton Press; P.O. Box 355; Newton, CN 06470 (bimonthly).

Goodfellow Review of Crafts; Box 4520; Berkeley, CA 94704 (bimonthly).

Handicrafts That Sell; Tower Press, Inc.; Box 428; Seabrook, NH 03874 (bimonthly).

The Quality Crafts Market; 521 Fifth Avenue; Suite 1700; New York, NY 10017.

Sunshine Artists, U.S.A.; Sun Country Enterprises, Inc.; 501 N. Virginia Avenue; Winter Park, FL 32789 (monthly).

Tole World; Daisy Publishing Company, Inc.; 429 Boren Avenue, North; Seattle, WA 98109 (monthly).

Workbench; Modern Handcraft, Inc.; 4251 Pennsylvania Street; Kansas City, MO 64111 (monthly).

American Art Journal; Kennedy Galleries, Inc.; 40 W. 57th Street; 5th Floor; New York, NY 10019 (quarterly).

Shuttle, Spindle & Dyepot; Handweaver's Guild of America; 65 LaSalle Road; P.O. Box 7-374; West Hartford, CT 06107 (quarterly).

Stained Glass; Stained Glass Association of America; 21 Tudor Lane; Scarsdale, NY 10583 (quarterly).

Studio Potter; Box 172; Warner, NH 03278 (semi-annually).

Appendix D

STATE OF _____

COUNTY OF _____

COMMISSION AGREEMENT

This Agreement, is made and entered into on the _____ day of _____

_____, 19____, by and between _____,

Artist, of _____, _____, (here-

inafter "Artist") and _____, of _____

_____, (hereinafter "Second Party").

WHEREAS, the Artist is a recognized professional Artist; and

WHEREAS, Second Party admires the work of Artist and desires to

commission the Artist to create a Work of Art in the Artist's own unique

style; and

WHEREAS, the parties wish to have the creation of the Work of Art

governed by the mutual obligations, promises, covenants and conditions

herein.

THEREFORE, for the considerations hereinafter mentioned, the mutual

covenants, conditions and promises herein contained, and for other good

and valuable considerations, mutual promises and undertakings, the suffi-

ciency and receipt all of which are hereby acknowledged, the parties have

agreed as follows:

1.

Artist agrees to perform all work required by the Contract

Documents (same being incorporated herein and made a part by reference) for the creation, design, purchase of materials, fabrication, transportation and installation of the Commission, titled "_____ _____".

The parties agree that Artist is an independent contractor, not an employee, that Artist is not being paid by the hour but according to the terms of this agreement; and that the Commission is not a work for hire.

2.

The Artist agrees to create the preliminary design for the Commission, if required, in the form of studies, sketches, drawings, models, macquettes or other examples as described in the Contract Documents in return for which the Second Party agrees to pay Artist _____ ($____) Dollars, as set out in Paragraph Seven (A) or (B). This amount shall be paid to Artist at time of execution and delivery of this Agreement unless special stipulations provide for progress payments.

Within two (2) weeks of receipt of the preliminary design, Second Party may demand changes, and the Artist shall make changes, as demanded, for an additional fee of $_____ per hour; provided, however, that the Artist shall not be obligated to work more than _____ hours to make changes.

Notwithstanding anything to the contrary herein, the Artist shall retain title and all rights to ownership and possession and have promptly returned the preliminary design, all incidental works made in the creation of the Commission, and all copies and reproductions thereof and the Commission itself, provided, however, that in the event of termination pursuant to Paragraph Eight (F), Second Party shall have the right to keep copies of the preliminary design for the sole purpose of completing the Commission, provided upon completion they shall be returned.

Title, possession, copyright and all rights of reproduction and all other rights to all models, macquettes, photographs and photographic slides shall at all times remain vested in the Artist.

3.

Parties agree that Artist shall begin work on the design as set out in Paragraph Seven and begin work on the Commission after receipt of written approval of the preliminary design, previous receipt of final and executed Agreement, including all Contract Documents and receipt of first payment of any sums required under Paragraph Seven. Subject to authorized delays and adjustments, Substantial Completion shall be achieved not later than _____. Time for substantial completion shall be extended by the number of days of delay caused by Second Party, or as set out in Paragraph Fifteen; Artist shall have _____ days grace period.

4.

Title to Commission shall remain in the Artist until Artist has received payment in full. In the event of termination of this Agreement pursuant to sub-paragraphs (A), (B), (C), (D), or (E) of Paragraph Eight, Artist shall retain title and all rights of ownership and possession in the Commission and shall have the right to complete, exhibit, and sell the Commission. In the event of termination of this Agreement pursuant to Paragraph Eight (F), Second Party shall own and possess the Commission in whatever degree of completion and shall have the right to complete, exhibit, and sell the Commission.

5.

Each Party gives to the other their permission to use the other Party's name, picture, portrait and photographs, if any, in all forms of media and in all manner, including but not limited to exhibition, display, advertising trade and editorial uses, subject to all provisions contained herein regarding copyright, and with no violation of either Party's rights of privacy or any other personal or proprietary rights they may possess in connection with reproduction and sale of the Commission, the preliminary design for the commission, or any incidental works made in the creation of the Commission.

6.

Second Party shall pay to the Artist the contract price of _____ _____ ($) Dollars, as set out specifically in Paragraph Seven, for all design and preliminaries, for performance of all work, including acquisition of all materials, labor and special work or services and installation as set out specifically in the contract documents. Artist agrees to notify Second Party if the Commission exceeds the contract price by written notice at least fourteen (14) days before completion. Any increase in cost resulting from delays covered by Paragraph Sixteen, by change orders requested by Second Party pursuant to Paragraph Nine, or by any other delays caused by Second Party, shall be paid for by Second Party.

7.

Second Party agrees to pay to Artist the contract price which shall consist of the total of:

a)   all design and preliminaries for the Commission,

b)   substantial completion of the Commission, and

c)   installation, special work and services, as follows:

a)(1)   Second Party agrees to pay to Artist the sum of _____

_____($____) Dollars, as payment for all design work. Balance in full is due and payable thirty (30) days from completion.

(2)   Second Party agrees to pay Artist, in advance, the additional sum of _____($____) Dollars, as payment for the production and completion of any models, maquettes or other constructions.

(3)   If this Agreement is terminated, any amounts that are unpaid, all costs and expenses incurred by Artist to date of termination shall be immediately due and payable by Second Party.

b)(1)   Second Party agrees to pay to Artist for substantial completion of the Commission in the sum of _____($____) Dollars, in progress payments, and on or before _____, 19___, Second Party shall pay to the Artist the sum of _____

_____($____) Dollars, which is payment of the first 1/3 of the sum due to the Artist for the Commission.

(2)   Upon completion of final design, purchasing of materials, assembling of equipment and fabrication of the individual members of the Commission, Artist shall make application to Second Party for payment by letter or on AIA Document 6702. (American Institute of Architects standard pre-printed

form available at most book stores.) Second Party shall have the right to inspect and approve progress within 7 days of the date of receipt of the application for payment. Within 14 days following the date of receipt of the application for payment, Second Party shall pay to the Artist the sum of _____ ($_____) Dollars, which is the second 1/3 of the sum due to the Artist.

(3) Upon substantial completion of the Commission, Artist shall make application for final payment by letter or on AIA Document 6702. Within 14 days following the date of receipt of the application for payment, Second Party shall pay to Artist the sum of _____ ($___) Dollars, which is the final 1/3 of the balance of the Contract Price due to the Artist. Delays in acceptance of the completed work, delays in installation, or rejection of the Commission in violation of the terms of this Agreement shall not relieve Second Party of the obligation to pay the Artist in full.

c) Second Party agrees to pay to the Artist the sum of _____ _____($___), as payment for installation of the Commission and the additional sum of _____ ($_____), as payment for special work or services on the Commission required by contract documents or special stipulation.

8.

The Parties agree that this Agreement may be terminated upon the occurrence of any of the following conditions:

A) If Second Party does not approve the preliminary design created by Artist pursuant to Paragraph Two, then the Artist shall receive all amounts payable for the preliminary design and shall keep all payments made and the Agreement shall terminate;

B) Second Party may, upon payment of any progress payment due pursuant to Paragraph Seven, or upon payment of an amount agreed upon in writing by the Artist to represent the prorated portion of the Contract Price due in relation to the degree of completion of the Commission, terminate this Agreement. The Artist hereby agrees to give promptly a good faith estimate of the degree of completion of the Commission if requested by the Second Party to do so;

C) Artist shall have the right to terminate this Agreement in the event the Second Party is more than sixty (60) days late in making any payment of the Contract Price due to Artist pursuant to Paragraph Seven: provided, however, that nothing herein shall prevent the Artist from bringing any lawsuit based on the Second Party's breach of contract or nonpayment;

D) Second Party shall have the right to terminate this Agreement if, a delay under Paragraph Three or Sixteen, or an illness of the Artist causes a delay of more than six (6) months beyond the completion date, or if events beyond the Artist's control cause a delay of more than one (1) year beyond the completion date; provided, that the Artist shall return any payments made pursuant to Paragraph Seven for work which was not completed and Artist shall not be liable for any additional expenses, damages or claims of any kind based on a failure to complete the Commission;

E) Second Party shall have the right to terminate this Agreement, except as otherwise provided, if the Artist fails without cause to complete the Commission within ninety (90) days of the completion date established in Paragraph Two. In the event of termination under this sub-paragraph, the Artist shall return to Second Party all payments made pursuant to Paragraph Seven, but shall not be liable for any additional expenses, damages or claims of any kind based on a failure to complete the Commission

F) This Agreement shall automatically terminate on the death of the Artist, provided, however, that the Artist's estate shall retain all payments made pursuant to Paragraph Seven for all work that has been completed

G) The exercise of a right of termination under this Paragraph shall be in writing and must set forth the grounds for any termination.

9.

The Parties agree that change orders may not be allowed unless expressed in writing, as amendment or modification to this Agreement, or to other of the Contract Documents. Second Party agrees to pay for any additional costs incurred for either materials, labor or other services related to each change order for any increase in costs caused by any delay resulting from a change order.

10.

The parties agree that all Contract Documents set out below are specifically made a part hereof and form a part of this Agreement, and shall be binding as to both parties. The contract document shall consist of and include the following:

a) Agreement

b) "BID", Models, maquettes, constructions, photographs, photographic

slides, drawings, renderings and studies by Artist for Commission.

c) Specifications and samples of materials

d) Technical requirements:

   i) Location

  ii) Size, color and weight

 iii) Other

e) Miscellaneous Services*

   i) Interior/Exterior lighting

  ii) Interior/Exterior site preparation

 iii) Installation

f) Change orders/amendments

g) Labor Union/Guild requirements

h) _____

11.

Artist shall supervise and direct all design work, fabrication and installation, using their best skill and attention, and they shall be solely responsible for all construction means, methods, equipment, techniques, sequences and procedures and for coordinating all portions of the Commission under the terms and conditions of this Agreement except as otherwise provided herein.

---

*Should any work on the Commission, including installation, require outside engineering, moving or other miscellaneous services not bid and included herein, then all costs for miscellaneous services shall be authorized by Second Party and billed directly to Second Party. Artist shall not be held responsible for any delays resulting from any required outside engineering, moving or other miscellaneous services not included in this Agreement.

12.

Unless otherwise specifically provided in the Contract Documents, Artist shall provide and pay for all labor, materials, equipment, tools. construction equipment and machinery, water, heat, utilities, transportation and other facilities and services necessary for the proper execution and completion of the Commission.

13.

Artist shall at all time enforce strict discipline and good order among employees and shall not employ on the Commission any unfit person or anyone not skilled in the task assigned to them.

14.

Artist warrants to Second Party that all materials and equipment incorporated in the Commission will be new unless otherwise specified, and that all work will be of good quality, free from faults and defects and in conformance with the Contract Documents.

15.

Unless otherwise provided in the Contract Documents, the Artist shall include in the bid where required and pay all sales and other similar taxes

Second Party shall advise Artist of, secure and pay for any building permits, any zoning variances, and all other permits and government fees, licenses and inspections necessary for the proper execution, completion and installation of the Commission. Second Party shall advise and notify Artist prior to entering into this Agreement of any and all requirements or provisions that have to be met pursuant to any labor agreement, union or guild organization.

Second Party shall afford the Artist reasonable opportunity for the introduction and storage of materials and equipment for execution, completion and installation of the Commission, and Second Party shall coordinate work on location for installation as required by the Contract Documents.

16.

If Artist is delayed at any time in the progress of the work, completion or installation of the Commission by any change order requested by Second Party, by fire, earthquake, flood, epidemic, accident, explosion, casualty, labor dispute or controversy, civil disburbance, act of a public enemy, embargo, war, Act of God, failure of or delay in transportation, adverse weather conditions, or any failure, without fault, to obtain materials or services essential for the completion and installation of the Commission, or any other cause beyond the control of Artist, or by any other cause which justifies the delay, then the Contract Time shall be extended for a reasonable time as Artist may require.

17.

Application for final payment shall include Artist's delivery to Second Party of a complete release of all liens or receipts in full covering all labor, materials and equipment for which a lien could be filed. Lien Release shall be in the form attached hereto and hereby made a Contract Document as part of this Agreement.

18.

The making of final payment shall constitute a waiver of all claims by Second Party except those arising from: (1) unsettled liens, if any; (2) faulty or defective Work appearing after Substantial Completion; (3) failure of the Work to comply with the requirements of the Contract Documents; or (4) terms of any special warranties required by the Contract Documents. The acceptance of final payment shall constitute a waiver of all claims against Second Party except those previously made in writing and identified by the Artist as unsettled at the time of the Application for Final Payment.

19.

Second Party agrees that in the event of any damage to the Commission, Second Party shall consult Artist prior to commencement of any repairs or restoration and if practical Artist shall be employed to make any required repairs or restoration, provided agreement can be reached for services of and payment to Artist.

20.

The Parties agree that the Commission is a _____ _____, (painting, sculpture, drawing, work of graphic art, such as an etching, lithograph, offset print, silkscreen print, seriograph, photograph, or crafts, such as crafts in clay, textile, fiber, wood, plastic, glass or similar materials) fixed in a tangible form. Artist reserves all right, title and interest in and to the copyright, the common law copyright if any, the statutory copyright, the right to apply for copyright registra tion, and any extensions and renewals thereof, the common law and statutory copyright in any publication, reproduction or other derivative rights of the work. Second Party has purchased an original Work of Art and the rights of Second Party shall be limited thereto and shall specifically not include television rights, theatrical rights, home movie rights, merchandising rights, use of title rights, publication rights, foreign edition rights, any and all reproduction rights, or other derivative work rights.

21.

The Parties agree that there must be affixed by Artist to the Commission a Copyright Notice, which shall include the copyright symbol, the name of the Artist and the date; it must be affixed to the work prior to any publication sale or display and the copyright notice shall be attached either to the Commission, to the frame or base, or adjacent thereto, all in a manner so that the notice shall be visible in a manner and location as to give "reasonable notice" of the Artist's copyright in the Commission. Any authorized use or reproduction of the Commission by either Party, for whatever purpose, shall include the Copyright Notice so that the rights of the Artist to the copyright will be protected.

22.

Second Party shall be responsible for purchasing and maintaining liability insurance and, at their option, may maintain insurance as will protect them against claims which may arise from operations under the Agreement.

23.

Unless otherwise provided, Second Party shall purchase and maintain property insurance upon the Commission at the site to the full insurable value thereof. This insurance shall include the interests of Second Party, Artist and subcontractors in the Commission and shall insure against the perils of fire and extended coverage, and shall include "all risk" insuranc for physical loss or damage including, without duplication of coverage, theft, vandalism and malicious mischief.

24.

The Parties waive all rights or claims against each other for damages caused by fire or other perils or personal injury to the extent covered by insurance obtained pursuant to terms herein or any other property, liabilit or other insurance applicable to the Commission, except rights or claims as they may have to the proceeds of any insurance held by Second Party.

25.

All notices and other communications hereunder shall be in writing and shall be deemed to have been given when delivered or mailed first class, postage prepaid, addressed to either party as set out above, or as they may otherwise designate in writing.

26.

If any term, covenant or condition of this Agreement be invalid or unenforceable, the remainder of this Agreement shall not be affected thereby, and the remainder shall be valid and enforceable to the fullest extent permitted by law.

27.

This Agreement and the Contract Documents attached hereto embody and contain the entire agreement and understandings of the parties and shall be binding upon and inure to the benefit of and be enforceable by their respective heirs, legal representatives, successors and assigns.

28.

This Agreement may be amended, waived, discharged, modified or terminated only by an instrument in writing signed by both parties.

29.

This Agreement is entered into in the State of _____, contains covenants to be performed within the State of _____ and shall be construed in accordance with and governed by the laws of the State of _____.

30.

Time is of the essence, except as otherwise provided.

IN WITNESS WHEREOF, the parties have caused this Agreement to be executed along with all necessary contract documents this _____ day of _____, 19_____.

_____(SEAL)
ARTIST

_____(SEAL)
SECOND PARTY

STATE OF _____

COUNTY OF _____

<u>BID</u>

I.   Description of Work of Art for Commission

II. Contract Price

    a)   design: _____

    b)   commission: _____

    c)   installation: _____

    other: _____

III. Other

_____
ARTIST

_____
SECOND PARTY

Appendix E

STATE OF _____

COUNTY OF _____

RELEASE OF LIEN

Artist states that all labor, services and materials required by the Agreement, and attached Contract Documents, for the Commission, or used in the construction of the Commission, have been fully and completely paid for; and that all work, labor, services, and materials were furnished and performed at Artist's instance.

Artist further states that the Commission has been completed in accordance with the Agreement contract documents.

Artist makes the above statements for the purpose of inducing Second Party to make final payment pursuant to their Agreement.

Artist further states that they claim no lien whatsoever on the Commission, and does release, acquit and forever discharge _____ _____ from and against any and all claims, debts, demands, or cause of action that the Artist has or may have as a result of furnishing labor, services and materials for the Commission.

The undersigned further states that there have been no other written assignments of any lien claimed against the above described property.

This _____day of_____, 19____.

_____(SEAL)
ARTIST

ACKNOWLEDGEMENT

Before me, the undersigned authority, personally appeared _____

_____, Artist, who after being duly sworn,

on oath, did acknowledge they executed the foregoing Release of Lien as

their free and voluntary act and deed.

Witness my hand and seal of office on this _____day of _____

_____, 19_____.

_____(SEAL)
Notary Public

Appendix F

STATE OF _____

COUNTY OF _____

AGENT'S AGREEMENT

THIS AGREEMENT, is made and entered into on the _____ day of _____

_____, 19___, by and between _____,

Artist, with principal place of business located at _____

_____, and _____

_____, (hereinafter "Representative"), with principal

place of business located at _____

_____.

WHEREAS, Artist wishes to create and sell _____

and other works of art, and desires the assistance of Representative to

assist with sales and with all business related thereto according to the

terms and conditions set out herein; and

WHEREAS, Representative wishes to represent and assist Artist, and

desires to use their best efforts to sell Artist's _____

_____ and other works of art, and to assist Artist in all business related

thereto;

NOW, THEREFORE, for the considerations hereinafter mentioned, the

mutual covenants, conditions and promises herein contained and for other

good and valuable considerations, the sufficiency and receipt all of which are hereby acknowledged, the parties have agreed as follows·

1.   Term.   This Agreement shall be in effect for a period of five (5) years from the above date unless sooner terminated as provided below or in paragraph Eight.

This Agreement may be terminated by either party by written notice to the other of termination.   All commissions due and payable to the Representative shall continue to be paid until same are paid in full.

This Agreement is based upon the personal relationship of the parties and shall terminate upon the death of either.   No assignment of this Agreement shall be made by either party without the consent in writing of the other party.

2.   Artist's Duties.   During the period covered by this Agreement, Artist agrees to create, produce and complete _____ and other works of art for sale, and to create, produce and complete any and all commissions and other commissioned works of art due to the efforts and representation of Representative.

3.   Representation Terms.   Artist agrees to establish, appoint and engage Representative as an independent contractor to represent Artist for the purpose of selling the Artist's _____ and other works of art and to secure commissions for Artist.   The parties specifically agree Representative is an independent contractor, and that this is not a consignment agreement, an agreement for direct purchase by the Representative, or an agreement creating for Representative an exclusive agency with Artist reserving the right to make sales without paying a commission, but an agreement granting Representative an exclusive right to sell the work of Artist; the Representative is granted the right to a

commission on all sales made by anyone, including the Artist, during the term of this agreement, except as otherwise provided herein.

The rights granted to Representative are limited to the 50 states of the United States of America.

Representative shall represent the Artist in locating commissions, shall present Artist's work to secure commissions, and shall negotiate contracts for commissions with the assistance of Artist on a commission contract acceptable to the Artist and Representative. Representative shall maintain contact with Purchasers, service and follow up on all sales and contracts for commission with Purchasers on behalf of the Artist for all business matters related to sales and contracts, and do all other acts that will promote the work and the sales of the Artist's work.

4. Payment. Artist agrees to pay to the Representative for all services rendered as follows:

a) If Artist requests Representative to work in the nature of advice, consultation and business for which there will be no commission or other remuneration, yet the Artist needs or requires the help and representation of Representative, then the parties shall agree in writing upon terms of payment by which the Artist will pay Representative; but Representative's duties to Artist include the promotion of Artist's work, that is considered part of their responsibility and duty to the Artist, and that promotion is specifically excluded from this provision to the extent that their representation and promotion of the Artist is their responsibility to the Artist as provided herein;

b) The parties recognize that Artist has been in business for some time, has a reputation as a _____, has completed commissions for certain purchasers, and has representatives in other cities and states, all of whom may contact or make inquiry to Artist regarding _____ _____or other works of art. The parties agree that in the event any inquiry is made directly to the Artist, then the Artist will refer the inquiry to Representative. Representative must be paid a commission for any sale as provided above in Paragraph Three. Any and all sales made directly by the Artist will be promptly reported to the Representative and payment made as provided below, provided the parties may agree that the Representative can negotiate the commission to be paid them or agree upon a split of any commission when the inquiring party is an Art Dealer/Collector or Gallery.

The parties agree that some exceptions may be necessary for Artist's previous customers, authorized Representatives or any other Gallery representing the Artist, however, the exceptions will be limited to those on the list attached hereto and no others will be allowed without further written agreement of the parties.

The parties acknowledge that Artist is dependent upon sales of Works of Art for a living and Artist must receive a certain amount of income from sales or their work each year for their livelihood, therefore, the parties agree that the Artist shall have no responsibility to pay commission to the Representative on direct sales made by the Artist unless Representative has made sales of Artist's work which guarantee the Artist _____ _____($) Dollars net income annually from sales of Artist's work. For purposes of this provision, sales shall be computed on a calendar for year basis. Any commissions on direct sales by Artist or commission on other sales, obtained by Artist and not excluded by the Artist, that are payable to Representative will not be due and payable to Representative until December 31 of each year unless otherwise agreed.

c)   The parties agree for future _____, or other future Works of Art, that are sold by Representative, or commissions that are obtained by Representative, Artist agrees to pay to the Representative for their services a commission of _____ per cent of the sales price.

d)   The parties agree for fully completed and existing _____ _____, or other fully completed and existing works of art by Artist that are sold by Representative, Artist agrees to pay to the Representative a commission of _____per cent of the sales price.

e)   All commissions, (except direct sales as provided in b) to be paid by the Artist to the Representative are to be paid within thirty days of receipt if sales price is received by the Artist; if sales price is received by Representative, then the sales price, less any commission, shall be paid within thirty days to the Artist; and all installment payments, progress payments or other credit payments shall be paid to the parties in direct proportion to the percentage of the sales price that is due to either party from the sale.

f)   Representative's commission shall be earned, due and payable upon receipt of full payment of the sales price (except for installment sales), or prevention of sale to a Purchaser who is ready, willing and able to purchase for the agreed sales price by default of Artist, including withdrawal from a sale, or the sale, transfer, assignment or rental of the _____ _____ or other Work of Art without the written consent of the

Representative.

5. Warranty. Artist warrants the originality of their works of art, absence of infringement of privacy or copyright of third parties and unencumbered title.

6. Limitations of Representative Rights. The parties agree that Representative has a fiduciary relationship to the Artist and owes a duty to the Artist to deal fairly and honestly, to care prudently for and to manage the business affairs for the Artist on sales contracts for commission, to account periodically and to disclose all information relevant to the representation of Artist. Representative agrees not to seek any benefit at the expense of the Artist.

The rights of the Representative in representing the Artist and in selling the work of the Artist shall be limited to the terms and conditions of this Agreement, and shall specifically not include television/video rights, newspaper, magazines or other printed matter rights, merchandising rights, use of title rights, publication rights, foreign edition rights, reproduction rights, derivative work rights and rights of public display. This Agreement is not intended to transfer any rights of copyright to the Representative, but rather, is an Agreement for Representative to represent Artist in the procurement of and completion of contracts for commission and for the sales of _____ and other works of art by Artist.

7. Copyright. Artist hereby agrees to provide Representative with all materials necessary to assist Representative in their efforts, including but not limited to photographs, prints, photographic slides, reproduc-

tions, publications, resumes, list of collections, and other similar materials useful to Representative. Artist shall be responsible for notifying the Representative of all known news or publicity about the Artist or the Artist's work, shows, exhibits, public displays or other events about the Artist or the work of the Artist.

The Representative shall use their best efforts to prevent the unauthorized copying, duplication, or publication of any Work of Art by Artist by any other party. All Works of Art and reproductions for any advertising, catalogs, or other publications for the promotion of exhibition or Artist's work shall be copyrighted, shall include the correct copyright notice and shall credit the Artist. Representative shall keep safe and secure all photographs and materials and upon expiration or sooner termination of this Agreement shall return all Works of Art, property and materials to the Artist.

8. Conflicts. The parties agree that the Representative may represent other Artist, but shall not represent another artist who is in competition with the Artist on any specific project unless Artist has declined participation in the project or unless it is with the consent in writing of the Artist. It is agreed between the parties that the Artist may request Representative to discontinue representing another Artist who is in direct competition with Artist as the alternative to termination of this Agreement, but Artist reserves the right to terminate this Agreement.

9. Arbitration. In the event a dispute arises under this Agreement, the parties shall confer with all reasonable dispatch in an endeavor to arrive at a solution; failing agreement, the dispute will be submitted to

a single arbitrator agreed to by the parties, or one appointed by the American Arbitration Association, who shall decide the dispute under the rules of the Association, and any Arbitrator's decision shall be final and binding upon both parties.

10. Notices. All notices and other communications hereunder shall be in writing and shall be deemed to have been given when delivered or mailed by first class, postage prepaid, addressed to the party as set out hereinabove, or as they may otherwise designate in writing.

11. Invalidity. If any term, covenant or condition of this Agreement be invalid or unenforceable, the remainder of this Agreement shall not be affected thereby, and the remainder shall be valid and enforceable to the fullest extent permitted by law.

12. Integration. This Agreement embodies and contains the entire agreement and understanding of the parties and shall be binding upon and inure to the benefit of and be enforceable by their respective heirs, legal representatives, successors and assigns.

13. Amendment. This Agreement may be amended, waived, discharged, modified or terminated only by an instrument in writing signed by both parties.

14. Time. Time is of the essence in each and every respect hereof.

15. Governing Law. This Agreement is entered into in the State of _____, contains covenants to be performed within the State of _____ and shall be construed in accordance with and governed by the laws of the State of _____.

16. Special Stipulations. If the following Special Stipulations

conflict with any of the foregoing printed provisions, the following
Stipulations are agreed to between the Parties and shall control over
any printed provision of this Agreement.

_____

_____

_____

_____

_____

_____

_____

     IN WITNESS WHEREOF, the parties have caused this Agreement to be
executed the _____ day of _____, 19____ .

_____(SEAL)
    ARTIST

_____(SEAL)
    REPRESENTATIVE

EXCLUSIONS PARAGRAPH (4)(b) AND PARAGRAPH 8

ARTIST:

          NAME   ADDRESS   DESCRIPTION

REPRESENTATIVE:

Optional

Special Stipulation #_____

Representative is engaged in the business of selling Fine Art and has built up and established a favorable and extensive reputation and trade in the business; Representative's business connections have been established and maintained at great expense and are of great value. Artist may obtain knowledge of Representative's business and acknowledges that the confidential information of the Representative includes customer lists, mailing lists, price lists, sources of supply, compensation arrangements, customer needs and methods of obtaining customers. Artist acknowledges that Representative will suffer great loss and damage if, after their termination, the Artist should for themselves or on behalf of any other person, persons, partnerships or corporations whom they may subsequently represent solicit business for sales of Works of Art from confidential information learned from Representative, or if they should use for their own benefit, or use for the benefit of or disclosures to others any confidential information learned during the duration of this agreement.

Artist agrees, acknowledges and covenants that Artist understands the nature, kind and character of the business of Representative.

In consideration of the promises herein made, Artist does expressly covenant and agree that during the term of this Agreement and for a period of _____(   ) calendar months immediately following termination of this agreement, that they will not in any manner whatsoever, for themselves or on behalf of others with respect to Representative:

(a) Call upon any person who has been a customer of Representative during the term of this agreement, but specifically excluding all customers of Artist prior to this Agreement;

(b) Compete, directly or indirectly, individually or as an officer, director, employee or partner or any person, firm or corporation with Representative in the _____, _____, area, and that they will not for this period in any way, directly or indirectly, compete with Representative in any type of business identical or reasonably similar to that of Representative;

(c) Furnish or divulge, directly or indirectly, the names of clients or customers or Representative, but specifically excluding new clients, or old clients of the Artist , brought to the Artist by the Representative.

(d) Disclose or furnish to any other person, firm or corporation, during the term of this agreement, or at any time during the future, the methods used by Representative, nor will they furnish to any person, firm or corporation a description of any of the methods of obtaining business, or advertising the same, or of obtaining clients, nor will they disclose to any person, firm or corporation any business information obtained by Artist during the term of this agreement with Representative.

Artist agrees that, in the event of breach or threat of a breach by Artist of this provision, that Representative shall be entitled to injunctive relief against any breach. No specifications, covenants or provisions in this Agreement shall be construed as a waiver or as a prohibition against Representative pursuing any other legal or equitable remedy against Artist as may be available under the laws of the State of _____

Artist specifically states that they have read this provision, that they understand the geographical areas which has been described that is restricted by this non-competing clause as well as understanding the length of time in which Artist cannot compete with Representative, and Artist further states and acknowledges that this provision as to non-competition has been carefully explained to them and they enter into this Agreement voluntarily with the understanding that this clause is contained herein, that they sign and execute this Agreement with knowledge of this provision and do so voluntarily and without protest.

Each restrictive covenant set forth is separate and distinct from every other restrictive covenant, and in the event of the invalidity of any covenant, the remaining obligations shall be deemed in full force and effect.

No termination by either party shall nullify the covenants and restraints set out except that they shall be of no force or effect should Representative cease doing business.

This the _____ day of _____, 19_____.

_____(SEAL)
ARTIST

_____(SEAL)
REPRESENTATIVE